# THE SILK ROAD TO

# International Marketing

## PROFIT and PASSION in GLOBAL BUSINESS

"Marketing is about relationships with global reach. You won't find a more discerning guide to forming and sustaining these complex webs."
– George S. Day, The Geoffrey T. Boisi Professor and Professor of Marketing, The Wharton School, University of Pennsylvania, Philadelphia

"Ambler and Styles have done an excellent job. Anyone attempting to conduct international business will recognize only too painfully the problems they identify – and will go on to be grateful for the solutions they describe."
– Martin Sorrell, Chief Executive Officer, WPP Group Plc

"An invaluable book, that brings the global v local debate up to date, and does so with insightful touches of observation and humour."
– Raoul Pinnell, Global Head of Brands and Communication, Shell

"*The SILK Road* brings a wholly new and fresh dimension to understanding international business. Packed with insights, devote your next plane ride to it."
– Professor John Quelch, Dean, London Business School

"Ambler and Styles show the way forward for those international marketers serious about winning. Expect to be inspired by this breezy 'must read'."
– Professor Sean Meehan, IMD, Switzerland

"Best book I've seen on the realities of international business and what it takes to be successful. Essential for all international marketers."
– David Fry, Business Planning Director, PepsiCo

"An indispensable guide to real world marketing. Great advice and great fun."
– Ted Niggli, Marketing Director, Procter & Gamble, Brazil

"In language at once formal, playful, and at times irreverent, Ambler and Styles place international marketing squarely within the emerging biological view of business success. Utterly refreshing!"
– Arie de Geus, Author of *The Living Company*

"None of the international executives I know spend their time hunched over figures: this *The SILK Road* is a great guide to what they really do."
– Javier Ferran, Regional President, Bacardi-Martini

# THE
# SILK
# ROAD
## TO

# International Marketing

## PROFIT and PASSION in GLOBAL BUSINESS

Tim Ambler
and Chris Styles

**FINANCIAL TIMES**
Prentice Hall

LONDON ■ NEW YORK ■ SAN FRANCISCO ■ TORONTO ■ SYDNEY

TOKYO ■ SINGAPORE ■ HONG KONG ■ CAPE TOWN ■ MADRID

PARIS ■ MILAN ■ MUNICH ■ AMSTERDAM

CATALOGUED

PEARSON EDUCATION LIMITED

Head Office:
Edinburgh Gate
Harlow CM20 2JE
Tel: +44 (0)1279 623623
Fax: +44 (0)1279 431059

London Office:
128 Long Acre
London WC2E 9AN
Tel: +44 (0)207 447 2000
Fax: +44(0)207 240 5771
Website: www.business-minds.com

First published in Great Britain 2000

The right of Tim Ambler and Chris Styles to be identified as authors of this work has been asserted by them in accordance with the Copyright, Designs and Patents Act 1988.

ISBN 0-273-64203-0

*British Library Cataloguing in Publication Data*
A CIP catalogue record for this book is available from the British Library.

10 9 8 7 6 5 4 3

Typeset by Northern Phototypesetting Co. Ltd, Bolton
Printed and bound in Great Britain by Biddles Ltd, Guildford & King's Lynn

*The Publishers' policy is to use paper manufactured from sustainable forests.*

# Contents

# Foreword

by Dennis Malamatinas, Chief Executive Officer, Burger King

In a world of copycats and commodities, this book is truly different.

It is the first I have seen that captures the essence of how international business really works, and it gets to the heart of what I believe drives success: people and passion. We all know that shareholder value is the bottom line, but it is the enthusiasm and learning that flows through human relations that gets us there.

When I look to those markets where we have our toughest battles and biggest successes, I notice it is always the people that make it happen – undaunted by the challenges and having fun getting the basics of fast food right. Our product has never been better and the gains Burger King is making around the world have never been more impressive.

Our people have turned the business around by their sheer passion for our brand and their professional commitment. They are no longer just counting the money. We used to sell franchises for the cash flow. Today we are dedicated to sharing and talking about the customers' experience. More than that, our people are dedicated to learning how other operations did well, and then doing it better. Many other world businesses can claim similar improvements but I have not read another book that so clearly explains why.

Reading it 35,000 feet up (as I suspect many others will), I immediately connected with the idea of the SILK road. The emphasis placed here on learning from our experiences, and each other, conjures up for me the need for our internal communications to stretch around the globe, and yet be smooth and seamless. And in our enthusiasm to embrace the new e-world and the many opportunities it brings, we are reminded here that while electronic connections will be invaluable to our efforts to enhance relationships, they cannot replace or replicate the "animal spirits" and shared learning that happen when people come together.

This book is also unique in the way it links individual experiences with creating a common purpose. Many of the concepts were new to me, too.

Now they seem obvious. The central observation that business is primarily social, but with economic outcomes, is something most of us know intuitively, but too often forget in our world of balance sheets, spreadsheets and so-called objective analysis. Rather than denying the obvious, we should be harnessing the power of our people and their passions, recognizing that wholly rational decision making is neither real nor desirable, and creating opportunities for shared learning.

The book also tackles the very real problems we face, and offers explanations and practical suggestions for addressing them. For example, there cannot be an international marketer anywhere who does not have to struggle with NIH (Not Invented Here). From time to time, I see some of our people, especially the successful ones, put up barriers to outside suggestions and no amount of intelligence, or emails, will bring those barriers down. We can send out as many directives as we like and they have no real effect. All that changes is a political deference to the prevailing wind.

When I was running Pepsi-Cola in Italy, and then Metaxa in Greece for International Distillers and Vintners, I probably exhibited the same tendencies. When I took charge of Smirnoff Vodka worldwide, I had to re-think my whole approach to getting the various countries behind my new global advertising campaign and global packaging design. The advertising agency, then Lowe and Partners, helped a great deal with the research and the rationale, but ultimately the nationals only joined in because they became partners in the process. We became a single team.

So I suppose, with hindsight, that we were engaged in information sharing, yes; but, more importantly, what these authors call animal spirits. Our purpose was obvious: we aimed to overtake Bacardi. What was not so obvious was that the qualities of our people would make the difference, not the calculations nor the increase in budgets that our parent company allocated. Particularly when those budgets had to be fought for with concerted determination and commitment. This also taught me how important, and difficult, it is to translate local points of view into world-wide action plans.

The only thing that bothers me about writing this foreword is the help it may give our competitors. But then we all benefit from a challenge. The better they will get, the better we will get. So I wish this book, and its readers all the very best. And remember that the key to success is unleashing the emotional energy of the organization to take you to a new and higher level. And with PASSION we will get to the winning post first, too. Enjoy it as I did.

# Acknowledgements

This book would not have been written but for our students, many of whom contributed thoughtful insights and many more who told us where we were wrong. They were both the inspiration and the taskmasters. Our next debt is to all the supportive friends, especially those who came to speak to the LBS Global Marketing courses, but also our colleagues at LBS and UNSW. Others fought their way through earlier drafts and helped reduce the verbosity. The complete list would be too long but at the certain risk of being unfair, we must mention Marvin Baker, Sir George Bull, Hugh Burkett, Tony Cooke, Arie de Geus, Ann Eastman, Sir John Egan, James Espey, Winston Fletcher, Barry Gibbons, David Hallam, Clive Holland, Keith Holloway, Don Knight, Dennis Malamatinas, Chris Nadin, Raoul Pinnell and John Stopford. Of course, we owe a great deal also to old colleagues at Grand Metropolitan and Procter & Gamble who, wittingly or not, provided so much of the reality which we hope separates this book from current international textbooks. Most of all we value their encouragement.

The Department of Trade and Industry (UK) and Austrade (Australia) generously funded our research on overseas market entry.

When we finally came to editing, Des Dearlove set us on the right path and then Bernie Ghiselin shouldered the main task of improving readibility.

At Financial Times Prentice Hall, we have been greatly helped by Pradeep Jethi pushing, driving and directing us (in the nicest possible way), Jacqueline Cassidy and Sarah Owens.

And finally, Katie and Linda who had to put up with those long hours when we communicated only with our computers.

To these and many more, we are eternally grateful.

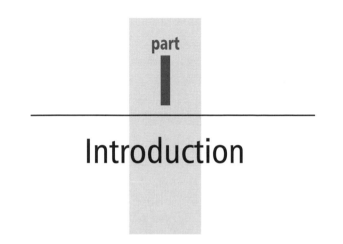

part

I

# Introduction

Few organizations are untouched by the imperatives of international marketing. Those who have not ventured overseas compete in their own backyards with foreign firms and brands. Moreover, a growing number of companies find themselves almost compelled to manage internationally. New technologies, of which the Internet and World Wide Web are only the beginning, are driving companies of all sizes, shapes and persuasions down the global road. From St. Louis to Savannah, from Seattle to Shreveport, small firms compete head-on with the large multinationals – and win.

In many cases, unfortunately, those managers with solid business education, but without international experience, find a yawning gap between the way the world works and the way its principles are conveyed in textbooks. In the classroom, a critical element – the human relationship – is almost completely ignored.

*The Reality.* Survival, profits, and growth in any organization depend on how well managers blend the personal and the relational with the analytical and rational, how well they instill the enterprise with spirit, with spontaneous, creative excitement. Those human talents of listening, empathy, learning, and open communications are major drivers of growth. Business is about feelings as much as it is about logic and quantitative analysis – perhaps more.

*The Textbooks.* Success in international marketing depends on the validity of data, on a well-crafted marketing plan, on the time-honored mathematical formulas that reveal the clear path to market share, on return on equity, and on shareholder satisfaction.

In *Profit and Passion* we offer a new understanding of how the international marketer adds value to the organization by blending the relational with the analytical. We have long known that relationships, "interpersonal skills," are crucial. Most good business schools do include some soft skill building in their programs; but this flavoring is peripheral to the hard logic of business realities. What do those intrepid MBAs find in the real world of organizations? That their instruction fell short. An entire dimension of practical, yet critical, understanding received but a gloss.

We seek to bring practice and theory, affect and cognition, together – quite literally. We believe both the relational and the rational are necessary, that neither is sufficient in guiding decisions. Our models do give salience to the former. In today's world, all formulas, equations, and theories must yield a major share of the limelight to qualitative, gooey, unmeasurable talents such as trust, empathy, motivation, self-awareness. Animal spirits not only stand side-by-side but absolutely drive the use and understanding of demographic, econometric, financial, and survey data. In this new universe, emotional intelligence precedes cognitive intelligence. Business is first biological, and only then logical.

Thus we begin.

In setting out to explain how international marketing works – and how it will work better – we make no distinction between "marketing" and "doing business." We are concerned with how organizations, large or small, gain and keep customer preference and thereby make money. The principles that apply to the Fortune 500 companies also apply to not-for-profit marketing: audiences must be identified and then satisfied before the organization can achieve its own objectives. In all cases, the international manager seeks to build the firm's market-based assets, which some call brands, while ensuring that short-term results are at least satisfactory. Whatever one's personal business orientation, the fact is that wealth is first generated in the market-place. The customers provide the cash.

*The principles that apply to the Fortune 500 companies also apply to not-for-profit marketing: audiences must be identified and then satisfied*

And building customer desire to provide that cash, the market-based asset, comes before the cash provision.

We address all types of international business, whether conducted by newcomers or veterans, by small firms or multinationals. Of course, there are differences between beginners and old hands, between large and small businesses, and between sectors. Multinationals have complex structures which both help and frustrate their managers, whereas small businesses have to operate in the uncertain world of "virtual multinationals," where the relationships are informal.

## National versus international understanding

Why should international differ from national marketing? First, while national marketing operates *within* markets, international operates *between* markets, seeking to ensure that the return to the company is greater than the sum of its national components. Why else support the costs of the international superstructure?

Second, each views its terrain from different angles. National marketing keeps its gaze at ground level and within defined boundaries. It assumes this view is unique and is receptive only to information that originates from within those boundaries. The international marketers rise above the local beliefs that their markets are unique. At ground level, the hills and valleys are obvious and seem impassable. But to the international marketers, looking down from their passenger jets, the land seems flat. Germany looks like Tennessee; Thailand looks like Georgia.

Each perception, or attitude, is correct in its own way. Perspective is dictated by the level of the perceiver; thus altitude determines attitude toward cross-border learning. Some companies call the ability to operate both at ground and higher levels "helicopter management." As we will see, success involves reconciling both views. International businesses should recognise the differences and profit from the similarities.

Because the global versus local question is with us to stay, reconciliation of the two perspectives is critical. Since most firms lack methods to resolve these disparities, marketing is often characterized by a certain ambivalence. The pendulum of strategy swings to and fro, first the global, next the local, then over to the regional, and back again. Reconciling these disparities involves ever more complex flows of information, co-ordinating systems within systems. With these complexities comes a natural resistance to information that fails to confirm stereotypes, plans, and established priorities. New tools of communication such as e-mail and voice-mail certainly help, as does affordable travel, but they do not automatically resolve the differences.

The Italian market can, technically, be run from Berlin or the Mexican business from Miami. Why then does national management need to be in the country and, conversely, why do international managers continue to travel when they could communicate from home? Simply because social information, the relational touch, is needed to bridge early gaps in understanding, and create the synergy between people that will transcend inevitable conflicts and difficulties along the way. This social element produces the need for a richer analysis than is offered by traditional formulas and models.

This is novel, yes, why else would you want to read it? In taking this leap, we bring together well grounded concepts from numerous sources as well as solid experience – our own and that of many others. Both authors were international marketers before they became academics. When we could find no suitable textbook to teach what we had lived, this book was born. It sets out to make sense of the experience all international business people share, and in so doing, explain what they do, and why.

## Business is (bio)logical

For centuries the dominance of rational analysis has blinded us to the social dimensions of business. Twentieth century business teaching has placed the quantitative above human interaction and learning to an astounding degree. From Frederick Taylor and time-and-motion analysis at the dawn of the century to most micro-economics today, humans have been assumed to be ultimately rational. Markets, despite all evidence to the contrary, are treated as logical. We are only constrained by the lack of information, goes the belief. Now that computers process more information than we can possibly handle, the fallacy is becoming exposed: exciting ideas that create value come not from logical machines, but from the human imagination nourished by social information.

Since Descartes we have been taught that our instincts, our "animal spirits," are suspect, that rational analysis is the higher order, perhaps the only order, of existence. Along with this philosophy came many assumptions: that thought is formal, just as mathematics is formal, that all thought is conscious, and that the mind can know its own ideas with absolute certainty. It was, in the words of Damasio, "The separation of the most refined operations of mind from the structure and operation of a biological organism." Western (but not Eastern) business inherited this notion that decisions are made – and should be made – in a way that is removed from the affective, the interpersonal life of the organization. Adam Smith encouraged the idea that business is fundamentally rational.

Since the mid-1970s the cognitive sciences have slowly undermined the view of mind and body as independent. From studies of brain-damaged patients, for example, neuroscience is showing that affective processing links with decision making in the ventromedial prefrontal cortices of the brain. These, as well as studies in linguistics and neural modelling, show the mind is inherently embodied, that thought is mostly non-conscious, and that abstract concepts are largely metaphorical.

This de-emphasis of the cognitive as the primary governing agent of human behavior brings into the foreground a new appreciation of relationships and feelings as agents of discovery. While this application of neurobiology to business remains in its infancy, the findings to date lend strong support to an organic understanding of business. Herbert Spencer, the Victorian polymath, coined the phrase "the survival of the fittest" and proposed that organizations be seen as biological entities.[1] Arie de Geus championed the idea in *The Living Company* and a swelling literature describes the business enterprise less as a machine than as a living organism that obeys natural laws of adaptation, co-evolution, and emergence.[2] This biological view stresses shared vision over command and control, the synthesis of minds over divisions of labor, creativity over capital, and consumers over producers.

This change in business culture – dare we call it revolutionary? – has found expression among those entrepreneurs who are returning business to its ancient roots as naturally economizing entities. In many of these businesses, there are no budgets, no central planning, no job descriptions. They compete through resilience instead of resistance, through adaptation rather than control. While necessary for survival and growth, profits are not seen as ends in themselves. The principal currency is the human relationship, not money. Technology is used to distribute rather than consolidate authority.

In this book we refer to all purely rational or analytical models as "Cartesian." We do not suggest that analytical methods are wrong or unhelpful.

Many certainly have a place in running a business. But we do challenge the assumption that strictly linear, mathematical models lie at the core of good strategy. Unfortunately, many business people long for foundations – a desire that must be overcome. We provide frameworks to bridge the gap between the logical analysis and the biological realities of business we encounter day to day. This more balanced approach requires us to examine the experiential *and* the rational aspects of international business, to determine what works, and then to explain why.

## Business is social

From all this, we suggest, business is social with financial consequences. It is not *primarily* a financial entity. This carries profound implications for the way business is conducted. Of course, financial performance is necessary to maintain our social groups, otherwise we face closure and eviction. We are not setting shareholder value, or any economic model, *against* a social model. We are positioning Cartesian thinking within a social context. At the same time, for reasons we will show, *exclusive* Cartesian focus damages the health of corporations and their brands.

Market-places are blended from unique chemistries of human desires, aspirations, relationships, feelings, as well as financial capabilities. If customers were robots, then marketing based wholly on rational analysis would make sense. But they are not. They are human beings – with all our a-rational ways. It is time, now, to understand the wider realities.

If any event symbolized the end of the Cartesian era, it was the mourning that followed the death of Princess Diana. No amount of hard logic could have predicted the outpouring of feelings triggered by her death. The usually staid British flocked to the streets by the millions to express their grief. They had to *act* in order to express *feelings*. No one anticipated the impact her death would have. She was no saint. Was it rational to wait ten hours in the rain to sign one of 200 books of condolence? Neither was this event unique: Eva Peron was more powerful in death than in life.

From this biological view of the organization, from the idea that creativity and knowledge growth spring primarily from human relationships and human connectivity, three concepts lie at the center of our models:

- Social information as the primary building block for organizational learning and knowledge. This social information is *implicit*. More than a matter of words, it is the cumulative affect of personal expression, the voice tones, body gestures, sense of humor, context, personal idiosyncrasies, one-on-one and network relationships. The interpretation of *explicit* information, the data that can be recorded electronically, emerges from our understanding of this shared social and implicit experience.

- Concepts such as commitment and enthusiasm are hard to explain in logical terms. The smile that transforms a meeting from dour to constructive, that creates passion for the brand, the energizing vision, the excitement of unexpected discovery, are all what we collectively call "animal spirits," for reasons we later explain. These are the life forces that distinguish people from machines.

- A shared sense of unique purpose and identity provides direction. This is not the official, boilerplate mission statement. This may come from the vision of a charismatic founder but is more a non-verbal, experiential community of belief. It is what those made redundant after 30 years with the company most miss. In *Fortune*'s 1997 review of the best managed companies, this sense of purpose and identity was one of the top three distinguishing factors for the best companies.[3]

Say goodbye, then, to the mechanical models that have dominated twentieth century business thinking from Taylorism to re-engineering. The excitement of life, growth and achieving the impossible comes from feelings, social interactions and relationships, and those energies that Descartes, and then Keynes, called "animal spirits."

## Relationship marketing

In recent years, relationship marketing has been identified as filling the gap left by traditional marketing and marketing strategy. The traditional view evolved from micro-economics and the application of psychology to consumer behaviour. Textbooks appeared in the 1950s, of which the most famous was Jerome McCarthy's "4Ps" – selling the right Product at the right Price with the right Promotion (including advertising) in the right Place (distribution). This marketing mix has barely changed.[4] Textbooks following similar formats have dominated the teaching of traditional marketing in business schools for the past 30 years.[5]

Although the consumer is represented as king, or queen, traditional marketing has been largely producer-centered and analytic, focussed on what the marketer can do to maximise the firm's results. Little attention is paid to empathising with the customer, nor to dealing with competitive factors. We call this the "Math" aspect of marketing, since equations provide its language.

The concept of strategy dominated marketing teaching from the 1970s onwards. This recognised the key role of competition and the need for differential advantage. Pleasing the customer was less important than beating competitors. Texts were provided, for example, by Michael Porter and George Day.[6] Market share became the dominant metric. We call this "War." Equations were replaced by military analogies.

In all this, the consumer's interests became secondary. The 4Ps promoted what the firm had to offer, and strategy required differential advantage, but the firm's orientation was either to the bottom line or to destroying the competitors. The relational perspective of marketing re-emphasizes the primacy of the consumer, and of social networks in wealth generation. Consumers are not value-neutral, transactional, utility maximizers, but sentient, experiential beings. Viewed from the relationship perspective, companies are social groups with economic consequences, not vice versa.

In some respects, East Asian philosophy is better suited to marketing than linear (Cartesian) thinking. China may well have a greater influence on twenty-first century business than the US had on the twentieth. The new millennium requires both Western and Chinese approaches to business issues. Chinese concepts such as harmony, balance, and non-linear time are all relevant to international marketing, and especially *guanxi* (connections). A *guanxiwang* is a network of relationships. This perception of marketing long anticipated the relationship marketing now recognized in the West. In essence, relationship marketing needs "Empathy" with the customer, but call it love if you wish.

In our scheme, then, relational marketing requires war, empathy, and math, all three, but the greatest of these is empathy.[7] This triumvirate and the interplay between its elements influence every discussion in this text. It is the foundation for everything that follows.

Of course, successful marketing cannot be reduced to formulas. What works is copied, used, and then ceases to work, its cycle exhausted. Oversupply drives prices down and consumers look for differentiation and novelty. On the other hand, the sure routes to disaster are regularly rediscovered. Marketing is paradox; just as innovation is essential, so is consistency. While great marketing should mean never having to worry about the competition, the reality is that most marketing is less than great. One ignores competition at one's peril.

Unlike previous texts, we emphasize human relationships above all else. All of us know relationships matter in business, and then we ignore them by letting finance take precedence. The same old merry-go-round of planning cycles deadens imagination, and ritual planning rain dances engage energies that would be better deployed in the market-place. We show how.

## Structure of the book

International marketing books fall into two categories: most are breezy insights for the executive in a hurry; others are analytic texts for the business school student. We were told to decide which this book would be: one *or* the other. Since challenging received wisdom lies at the heart of good marketing, we asked, "Why not both?" Executives who read business books presumably do so seriously. Business school students are also people in a hurry. This then is a breezy book for serious people. References provide guideposts for those who wish to pursue particular issues in greater depth.

We begin by identifying typical problems met by international businesses, and for which classical Cartesian approaches provide little assistance. Experienced managers will be able to add their own examples. Against this backdrop, we build the frameworks of understanding. In Chapter 2, we discuss the network of value-adding relationships, which are the basic conduits for business. As noted above, this does not limit us to the large international groups. As links in virtual organizations, even small companies form relationships around the world. We are less concerned with structure than with what international marketers do. We use our own research sponsored by the UK and Australian governments to show which practices work. Much of this reverses traditional views of export priorities.

Chapter 3 explores how these relationships are used to share explicit and, perhaps more importantly, implicit information. We move from the way an *individual* deals with information to the *organization* as a whole. The recognition of opportunities, dimly seen at first, is shared implicitly before becoming codified to the point where it can be recorded or transferred in computer code. Indeed the process of conversion is the source of value. The

SILK framework posits that value, in part, and organizational knowledge arises from Social Information converted to organizational Learning and then to Knowledge.

Against that backdrop, we can better understand how marketing decisions are made. Both customers and managers use the same apparatus – the human brain. Modern neuroscience is discovering what we have long suspected: decision making owes more to habits, experience, and feelings than it does to reason. The question of whether that "should" be the case and whether more rationality enables a firm to do better misses the point: rationality, however desirable, takes place within the context of memory and feelings (affect). The individual decision-making model (*see* Chapter 4) is therefore labelled MAC, i.e. **M**emory sets the context for **A**ffect (the primary source of conscious decision making), which in turn provides context for **C**ognition (thinking), whether employed before or after the decision is actually made.

Chapter 5 returns us from the individual to the firm and positions planning as the key mechanism for organizational, and therefore cross-border, learning. In large firms, planning is disliked. It occupies too much time, it is unrelated to reality, and is used for (excessive) control. We need a revolution in management thinking to make planning fun. Rehearsing the future should liberate, not stifle, ideas. It should stimulate the sharing of solutions across the borders of function, division, country, and hierarchy. Planning should be a process which uses all three marketing paradigms in the following order: **W**ar, **E**mpathy and **M**ath (WEM). Reconnaissance and strategy (W) need to precede customer understanding. Relationships should give direction to actions (E), but if they do not add up to provide the firm's desired outcomes (M), the cycle needs to start again. You can rehearse the future as often as you like – but you will only live it once.

Relationships, information, and learning are important but not the vital, i.e. "living," component of international business success. We share with Arie de Geus and others (above) the concept that the organization is a biological organism. Thus, it depends on its life force as much as any other biological organism. An exhausted or sick organism can do no more than support its own systems; it cannot grow. Performance depends on energy and, in a word, passion. Chapter 6 uses one last acronym both to capture the crucial role of animal spirits and to link them with goals and information. Thus, PASSION stands for **P**urpose, **A**nimal **S**pirits, **S**ocial **I**nformation and **O**rganizational k**N**owledge (OK, we cheated).

Now, what about measurement? What is its place? Real world marketers are ambivalent. On the one hand, they see measurement as providing the professionalism modern business needs, especially in segmenting and understanding customers. On the other, they are less keen on their own performance being measured and publicly displayed. More to the point, however, they see the conflict between narrow analysis and intuitive ideation. Numbers and fixed equations are confining. Chapter 7 seeks a path through this minefield by providing a practical approach to marketing metrics across borders. Whatever the firm's approach to standardizing the global marketing mix (product, price, advertising and promotion), measurement needs to be harmonized. This enables cross-border learning which, in turn, is the main *raison d'être* for the international superstructure in the first place.

Let us agree. The multinational organization is a complex web of competing objectives and priorities. In theory, the enlightened, holistic approach to planning, supported by a common measurement system, will provide universal harmony and co-ordination. But in practice animal spirits at the local level, in the form of NIH (Not Invented Here), will frustrate cross-border learning. Most international executives report that this provincialism is the single largest obstacle they encounter. Yes, they want initiatives at the local level, but they also want them to be informed by initiatives elsewhere. Chapter 8 deals with particular aspects of international marketing: developing new products, speed to market, and advertising. The lessons apply equally to other parts of the marketing mix.

At the same time we must recognize the differences, especially those between sectors. Chapter 9 shows that these are not as great as they are usually taken to be. All sectors need to distinguish between their immediate buyers (or store managers in the chain retail business) and end users. We discuss sector differences and what adaptation needs to be made before moving on to consider the change that the digital revolution is making to international business practices in Chapter 10.

The last Chapter (11) reviews the post-Cartesian business world. Today's concern with life forces in business is not just a passing fad like so many fashionable management recipes. The Cartesian view dominated thinking for perhaps 300 years and has led to the mechanical models and computers of the twentieth century. Now we can leave rational data processing to computers and free our managers to do what computers cannot –

provide intuition, insights, social exchanges, and the passion for the business that drives performance. The biological era has replaced the Cartesian and it is here to stay.

# References

1. Spencer, H. (1873) *The Study of Sociology*. London: Kegan Paul & Tench.
2. de Geus, A. (1997) *The Living Company*. London: Nicholas Brealey.
3. The other two were personal leadership by the chairman/CEO and working facilities.
4. McCarthy, J. E. (1960) *Basic Marketing: A managerial approach*. Homewood, Illinois: Richard D. Irwin.
   McCarthy, J. E. and Perrault Jr, W. D. 1991 *Basic Marketing: A managerial approach*. Homewood, Illinois: Richard D. Irwin.
5. For example, Kotler, P. (1997) *Marketing Management: Analysis, planning and control*. 9th Edn, Upper Saddle River, NJ: Prentice Hall.
6. Porter, M. (1985) *Competitive Advantage: Creating and sustaining superior performance*. New York: The Free Press.
   Day, G. S. (1986) *Analysis for Strategic Management Decisions*. West Publishing.
7. Based on 1, Corinthians 13.

# One touch of nature

'One touch of nature makes the whole world kin,
That all with one consent praise new-born gawds,
Though they are made and moulded of things past,
And give to dust that is a little gilt
More loud than gilt o'er-dusted'

*Source:* William Shakespeare[1]

Like one in three French people, Sylvie and Pierre are divorced. Their parting was reasonably amicable: they see each other from time to time, they do their best for their daughter Chloe, eight, and they suffer occasional pangs of remorse that their marriage had to end.

Pierre, approaching 40, is a dreamer, a gentle, strong "new man." Sylvie, today's woman, is somewhere in her 30s. She is thrusting, successful, feminine, still believing, despite their separation, that Pierre is the only man in her life. You know, instinctively, that they will one day get together again. You know it because they both drink Nescafé Special Filtre.

Across the Channel, life is less wistful but more complex. It was at the dinner party in a boyfriend's London flat that Louise first met Mark … The on-again, off-again love story is punctuated by Nescafé Gold Blend.

The fictional lives and loves that were once sponsored by soap are now, in Britain at least, the virtual monopoly of coffee. Gold Blend saw sales rise by 40 per cent after the first 12 episodes, which were stretched over five years. The second series has raised sales a further 13 per cent. The Gold Blend paperback book reached the top 10 best-sellers list within five days of publication.

The Spanish translation of the first British series is now running in Central and South America and the subtitled English version is doing well in Scandinavia. Why has France made its own, Gallic version of the global saga? Marketing men will point out that France is the only other European nation with advertising as sophisticated as Britain's. True, there is a lot less humour and a lot more sexism and gratuitous nudity. But French viewers, like those in Britain, demand advertisements as challenging as television drama.

*Source: The Times* 3rd leader, 11 August 1995

---

If there is one reliable constant that plays across international markets, it is paradox.

As the story illustrates, Nescafé deals with this lack of consent as a matter of course. After some botched trials, it ran another version of the Gold Blend advertising in the US, but for another brand name – Taster's Choice. Here we have one of the world's most advanced international marketers unable to use the same advertising, or even the same brand name, in three of its leading markets. Why? Are consumers really that different? Or the opinions of their marketing managers? Or their ad agencies?

This, in capsule, is the dilemma faced by international business, whether in marketing or not. What is reasonable and predictable in one country produces anarchy in another. Some companies reconcile these differences by simple command. The authority wielded by Japanese companies, for example, stood them in good stead between 1960 and 1990. But their approach was more subtle than a stern "diktat" and followed intensive internal learning across borders of all kinds: functional, business unit, country, and hierarchy.

In the Western context, it is well to exercise restraint and not hand authority to international managers too soon. The better course is to relax, learn, and build relationships with international subsidiaries and distributors slowly. Frustrating as it may be, bring co-ordination through selling, not telling, develop the international team's understanding of local customs and situations until a bond is formed with national marketers.

If the globe truly were a single market, there would be, for whatever we are selling, one product, package, price, and set of communications. Conversely, if every country were totally different, none could learn from any other. There would be no role for international marketing. Nor any need for this book. The goal, we suggest, is "To make the whole world kin," with diverse solutions to similar problems. The way to achieve that goal is to play within, to appreciate and exploit that very lack of international consent.

## International marketing and paradox

International assignments are often stepping stones on the way to senior management. Sometimes they are a requirement. Both Ed Artzt and John Pepper handled Procter & Gamble's international operations before becoming CEO. Once appointed to the glamorous, jet-setting international assignment, however, the ambitious manager is faced with a number of conflicts that seem to get in the way of replicating past success. This book was motivated by these apparent paradoxes. Few textbooks acknowledge, let alone explain, them.

**Table 1.1    Some paradoxes of international marketing**

| | | |
|---|---|---|
| We are taught the techniques of rational analysis and decision making | BUT | So many decisions seem to be influenced by "gut feel" or personal whim |
| We rely on consumer research to guide our marketing activities and make forecasts | BUT | There is often a substantial difference between what consumers tell us they will do, and what they actually do |
| We are expected to innovate constantly | BUT | We are often forced to standardize across markets and adopt the ideas of others |
| There is no longer a shortage of data | BUT | There is still a huge shortage of insightful knowledge |
| With the new electronic means of connecting people, there appears little reason to travel | BUT | We travel – often vast distances for short meetings – more than we ever did |
| Successful domestic marketers are often rewarded with prestigious international assignments | BUT | Domestic marketers often don't do well internationally |
| We are expected to take advantage of the new global market-place | BUT | We must be responsive to local tastes |
| We are encouraged to build global brand assets for the long term | BUT | We have to keep our monthly (weekly?) sales and profit numbers up – regardless of any long-term impact |
| We devote large amounts of time to intricate planning | BUT | Our plans seem to have little relevance or use once written |
| We believe great strategy is the way to success | BUT | Success sometimes comes down to good luck |
| Superior product should help us replicate our success across markets | BUT | Our competitors and their local distributors consistently beat us |

To these paradoxes we can add quite a few questions.

The responsibilities of national and international managers can be divided in various ways, strategy versus tactics, short- versus long-term planning, for example. Is it a good idea to remove the opportunity for conflict through this kind of separation? Perhaps national managers should have profit responsibility, leaving the market-based asset (e.g. brand equity) responsibilities for international managers?

More broadly, how does the international management structure add value? Most large organizations have their equivalent of the seagull manager joke (fly in, make a lot of noise, fly off, leaving the locals to clear up the mess). No one questions the need for some central tax and accounting functions, but how do central strategy, business and marketing specialists earn their keep? After all, national managers could meet up and exchange notes without high level, and probably more expensive, players looking over their shoulders and second guessing them.

What drives global success? Is it organizational learning? Superior information? Some companies have appointed chief knowledge officers (CKOs) in addition to heads of information, finance, and accounting. The 1990s have seen large organizations seeking increased focus on core businesses and skills, buying what fits and selling what does not. But how will they get these newly merged companies to work together? Each has developed its own culture, ways of doing things, which provide their competitive advantage. Breaking up the cultures could destroy those advantages.

If superior decisions flow from securing superior information and processing it better, what should we be measuring? Should all markets measure the same things? If so, how can they react to different competitors in different places, consumer differences and innovations? Most multinationals have standardized accounting information, but that, partly as a result, may now be dominating non-financial measures.

Given the ambiguity, chaos, and rapid changes confronting the international manager, how should they budget their time? How much of their resources should be taken up by planning? By training and personal development, the activities of task forces and consultants? Quite often, task forces cannot get together because the members are attending other meetings. They are engulfed with information. They are all trying to drink from fire hydrants and have less and less time to do so.

How do you determine the health of your company and its brands? If they are sick, or just plain tired, what do you do about it? How do you measure brand equities internationally?

As the Nescafé example showed, innovation is transferred across borders with difficulty. What process can resolve disputes in such a way that local managers are motivated and committed to the success of "foreign" concepts and ideas? When Colgate-Palmolive sought to repeat, in Canada and the UK, the huge success Cleopatra soap had found in France, it proved disastrous. Were the consumers really that different?

Should one seek advertising convergence by appointing a single ad agency world-wide? Probably not. Should one seek a single set of brand tracking metrics by appointing one market research company world-wide? Probably yes. Why the difference? And are the answers to all these questions likely to apply in all companies in all sectors? Surely business is not that simple. If there were a set of good answers, why do successful managers from one company or sector often fail when transferred to another?

Some of these questions will resonate with the issues being faced today by your company. You may have other international business problems faced by your company. We suggest they can be categorized into three types: those that are not very significant and can be left to themselves; those that can be solved using classical analytic techniques; and, those that can be resolved using the more advanced frameworks in this book.

Before you read on, pause and make a record of what you consider the primary problems you face beyond the province of your national managers. If, by the end of this book, there are any that are not allocated to one of those three categories, please email them to tambler@lbs.ac.uk or c.styles@unsw.edu.au. We would be glad to learn of them.

# Reference

1. Shakespeare, W. *Troilus and Cressida*. Act III, iii, 175–179. London: William Collins (1902 edition), p. 773.

# Relationships for the long haul

'I do business with people, not companies'[1]

## Joint venture switches Adelaide firm on to growth

Hong Kong has been the setting for a stunningly successful joint venture with an Australian company, in a field littered with corporate culture clashes and mutual suspicion.

Adelaide-based Rob Gerard, whose father founded Gerard Industries, markets the Clipsal brand of electrical accessories and products. "I set out to make Clipsal the number one brand throughout Asia. I knew we couldn't do that on our own, so I set out to find a partner," he says.

The company had been dealing over lighting dimmers with a family business, Gold Peak Industries, then run by the four Lo brothers in Hong Kong. Gerard eventually became particularly close to the youngest brother, Victor, who is today chairman of Gold Peak, which is listed in Hong Kong.

Gerard said: "I kept chipping away with them, saying 'Why don't we work the Clipsal name up in Asia?' We launched the brand name in Hong Kong in 1977 – and are celebrating the twentieth anniversary on June 2."

Gerard supported the move with technical expertise, tool-making and personnel from Australia, and the Lo family looked after sales and market-ing, "which had to be done by Chinese people."

Markets were developed in China, Singapore, Malaysia, Indonesia and elsewhere in Asia, through an arrangement based on licensing and royalties. More recently, sales have been made in the Middle East, South Africa and elsewhere, pushing Clipsal into one of the top five electrical accessory brands in the world. Gerard believes it is now number three.

"I was 26 when I arrived in Hong Kong. Victor is six years younger. We had a lot of good times, and our business grew out of our initial friendship. Our biggest threat seemed to be from Asia; now we have created our own brand name within Asia," says Gerard. Australia remains the company's biggest market, and Gerard Industries employs 3,400 people there, mostly in Adelaide, producing $A400 million annual turnover.

Gerard adds: "The greatest lesson to come from this is that you can't do it on your own. Once you come to that conclusion, you must build a partnership. You might be able to handle the technology and help someone set up a factory, but your partner really needs to run the companies in Asia, employing the staff, handling the day-to-day business. People make too many mistakes trying to run companies in countries where they don't even understand the business characteristics."

"The secret is trust. That enables the relationship to work over thousands of miles. Victor Lo and I chat regularly on the phone."

*Source*: edited from *Australian Financial Review*, 29 April 1997, p. 31

---

Much has been written over the last ten years about the importance of personal relationships in business. Experienced managers are amused to find trust, commitment, and co-operation coming into academic fashion, or even being researched. They have long known the importance of lasting business friendships.

In emphasizing relationships we might be criticized for stating the obvious. Relationships stand at the foundations of international marketing. The very nature of business relationships, how to build good ones and monitor their progress, receives too little formal attention. A review of seven leading international marketing textbooks published in the 1990s reveals only three chapters that address relationship issues at length.[2] To succeed in the future world market-place business people will need to do more than note these issues. We need to dig deeper.

In modern international business, financial analysis often dominates planning. Pressures for short-term performance do not assess or account for the slow building of relationships. This is unfortunate. These relationships, such as that between Rob Gerard and Victor Lo, should become the central focus for resource allocation and for dictating what international managers actually do.

The one-to-one (dyadic) relationship has become the major building block of brand equity. The complex biological success model we develop in these next three chapters begins with the development of mutually rewarding, idea-sparking, personal relationships. While co-operation is the dominant mode, any relationship also includes some degree of competitive game playing. Indeed, that competition is necessary for its vitality.

## The nature of relationships

Those who conduct business in the oriental cultures of the Middle East and Asia observe little separation between business and private life – particularly when customers ring at 11 pm on a Friday evening. The nature of the relationship reflects this: you are friends before you can do business, and serious business is only done between friends.

Western cultures are vaguely uncomfortable with friendships in business and, on the surface, play them down. The rational rules the day. And yet, the camaraderie found at golf clubs, fashionable bars, among business school alumni, or neighborhood friendships, plays an important part in decision making. Senior executives are influenced by personal networks, peer pressures, group norms, and the wisdom of the nineteenth hole.

Recently, economics has sought to accommodate this reality. The dismal science now concedes that long-term relationships help lower transaction costs – the costs associated with the process of buying and selling – and improves efficiency through better inventory management and the exchange of data. Thus, for example, global auto makers have reduced their number of suppliers.

Other payoffs from relationships are more difficult to quantify. Trust, for example, is clearly both a result and a cause of a relationship. Common sense suggests that high-trust business relationships are more productive, creative, and efficient than low-trust relationships. But the future cash flow from trust is difficult to calculate. And misplaced trust can be expensive.

As a first step, we need to understand the key dimensions of a business relationship:

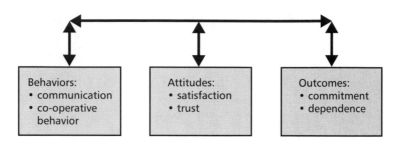

| Behaviors: | Attitudes: | Outcomes: |
| • communication | • satisfaction | • commitment |
| • co-operative behavior | • trust | • dependence |

**Fig. 2.1    Relational dimensions**

These dimensions carry different meanings, motivations, and outcomes.[3] Commitment, for example, can be based on an assessment of there being no better option ("calculative commitment"), or on personally liking the other partner ("affective commitment"). Relationships based on the former are not as secure as those which are dominated by the latter.

Trust includes many discrete components. We might describe them, but we have reservations about taking reductionism too far. A relationship is holistic. It is not a Lego toy which can be separated into pieces. But however described and measured, the kind of trust that exists between Victor Lo and Rob Gerard, is the foundation of most successful business partnerships.

Co-operation also has clear business implications for joint ventures, cross-licensing agreements, and other alliances. Year by year, formerly fierce competitors pool their resources. For example, IBM and Apple co-design computer chips, British Airways and Qantas code-share on the Australia to UK route. Regulatory watch-dogs in both the US and Europe are struggling to keep up.

Communication, the right kind at the right time, is critical. Given the technology at our disposal there is, in theory, no reason why we have to travel to communicate. But technology has not, and will not, replace the power of personal contact. High levels of trust are not built between people who have never met. In China, a fax to someone who does not know you will get no response. Until you appear in person, you do not exist. We learn the more powerful lessons through social interaction – as we discuss in Chapter 3. Electronics and improved airline timetables reduce distance. But spoken language and the non-verbal gesture are the tip of the cultural ice-berg. Trust and commitment rely on open and frequent communication and on shared cultural understandings.

On the surface, the complex "stuff" of relationships sounds ordinary, intuitive, needing little explication. But when it comes to long-term business relationships, such talents as trust, communication, and co-operation do not always come naturally to Westerners. Individualism and the imperatives of competitive advantage lead to an inbred resistance to sharing assets. How often in trust-building exercises do we see executives choosing the compet-itive, private gain option rather than a team, group, or network option? In the long term, whether in business or anything else, change and conflict are inevitable in relationships. Identity never remains fixed. The only way to resolve these conflicts, to adjust to new realities, is through robust, open dia-logue. Without trust, communications, and other interpersonal traits, that dialogue breaks down.

## Relationships and performance

But do good relationships predict business performance? Our research among British and Australian exporters suggests there are important pay-offs.[4] Specifically, higher business performance among exporters was found to be positively linked with:

- Co-operation with overseas distributors (in setting strategy, objectives and so on)
- Trust in the distributor
- Satisfaction with distributor performance
- Commitment to the relationship with the distributor
- An intention to maintain the relationship with the distributor
- Effort devoted to maintaining the relationship with the distributor

We also found that higher performing exporters communicated more with their distributors, as shown in Table 2.1.

Table 2.1    Communication and performance

| Means of communication | High-performing projects (n=236) | Low-performing projects (n=198) |
|---|---|---|
| Average phone calls per month | 22.1 | 14.6 |
| Average letters and faxes per month | 30.7 | 17.9 |
| Average visits to the distributor per year | 4.3 | 2.7 |
| Average visits from the distributor per year | 1.6 | 1.1 |

*Notes:*
The export projects studied were divided into performance ratings above and below the average.
The averages for high-performing projects are all significantly (p<0.05) greater than the averages for the low-performing projects.

An interesting question is whether high-trust, co-operative relationships lead to better performance, or vice versa. The answer is both – a virtuous, continuing cycle of improving relationship leading to better business, and better business leading to a better quality relationship. The Chinese typically enter this virtuous cycle in small, low risk, ways. As favors are returned the stakes increase.

The implications should be clear: managers should think of themselves first as builders of relationships – with customers, employees and suppliers – which can and should be examined along a number of relational dimensions. The better the quality of the relationship, the better the business is likely to be. We will revisit these dimensions, and their measurement, in later chapters.

## Forming and developing relationships

How, then, do we go about starting and maintaining these relationships?

We would suggest there is a step-by-step process that managers can follow, tracking their progress as they move along. Derived from social psychology, Table 2.2 shows how theory maps onto the reality of exporter/distributor relationships.[5] Relationships develop through phases that are initially behavioral, then increasingly attitudinal before outcome dimensions come into play.

**Table 2.2   The relationship formation process**[6]

| Relationship stage | Relationship formation | Exporter/distributor relationship development |
| --- | --- | --- |
| 1 Awareness/reputation | • Awareness that the other party could be a feasible partner<br>• Facilitated by proximity | • Exporter and/or distributor becomes aware that the other party could be a feasible partner<br>• Facilitated by proximity (trade shows and so on), prior social/economic ties |
| 2 Exploration/interaction | • Initial attraction<br>• Trial phase<br>• Low investment<br>• Communication/interaction begins | • Initial attraction from perceived potential and reputation<br>• Initial meeting between exporter and distributer<br>• Trial phase used to assess future potential and provide for the development of trust and performance expectations<br>• Parties communicate/interact – initially business oriented |
| 3 Expansion/evaluation | • Assessment of each party's satisfaction with the other's performance and associated rewards<br>• Greater risk taking due to increased trust<br>• Mutual dependence develops | • Relationship assessed on interaction experience<br>• Distributor is assessed in terms of satisfaction with performance and trust<br>• Mutual dependence develops |
| 4 Commitment/loyalty | • Relational continuity between the two parties<br>• High levels of inputs to the relationship | • "One business" mentality<br>• View relationship as long-term<br>• High levels of effort to maintain the relationship |
| 5 Dissolution | • Costs of continuing the relationship outweigh benefits | • Poor distributor performance<br>• Better alternative (including own company subsidiary) |

What are the implications?

First, starting a relationship with an overseas distributor does not usually happen by chance. Personal and family networks are important: 43 percent of the exporters we surveyed claimed first contact through either personal contacts or friends, or knowing the distributor from a previous job. Attending trade shows, seeking the help of "dating agencies," either government sponsored (via embassies) or private consultants, all can help.

> *It is better to choose an export market with poorer potential than a second-rate distributor*

There is the question, do you need a distributor at all? Maybe you can, within the European Union for example, keep it simple and sell direct to retailers. Conversely, should you engage several? A large embroidery machine maker in Beijing employed three distributors in each new market and then sacked the two that proved less successful.

Whatever the process, the selection of the right importer, or exporter, is more valuable than all the economic analysis since Adam Smith. It is better to choose an export market with poorer potential than a second-rate distributor.

Instead of using a general distributor, other options for the exporter include:

- Contracting a licensee
- Forming a shared-equity joint venture
- Manufacturing or assembly close to the market
- Acquisition
- Creating a wholly owned subsidiary

We follow convention in describing initiatives from the exporter's viewpoint, but the importer just as often makes the running.

Textbooks present sound analytical frameworks that lay out the costs and benefits of each entry method.[7] For example, marketing might be turned over to the distributor more substantially for simple products than for those that are technically complex. Export documentation, what a distributor does, Free Trade Zones and/or duty-free storage, and technical issues are all similarly covered and need not distract us now.

Companies usually develop each overseas market incrementally, mini-mizing *risk* at each stage.[8] Initial export sales may be made *ad hoc*, but then, as a pattern emerges, a single importer is contracted. Local manufacturing on a licensee or joint venture follows and ultimately the exporter sets up its own fully-fledged business in the export market.

The four main drivers of this evolution are:

- Control of local marketing to achieve consistency with strategic intentions and across borders

- Acquisition of incremental profit (i.e. the distributor's share) available from the owned brands in the territory

- Increase of corporate learning up from the distribution channels and then across from market to market

- Use of the strength of the exporter's leading brands to help the rest of the exporter's portfolio

Note the importance of learning from distributors, who are closer to end users. Of course, learning works both ways, but the sophisticated exporter does not seek to impose marketing policies until he knows his market.

We raise these future considerations at this stage because such a step-by-step developmental approach, while designed to minimize risk, carries a risk of its own. Importers have been through this process before. Why should they commit to an exporter who will only use them until a better option comes along? Issues of trust and commitment are crucial and reciprocal. Any firm considering progressive development as jumping in, and then out of, bed with the importer needs to review the options from its partner's point of view. Insecurity can easily derail the export drive at the outset.

*The sophisticated exporter does not seek to impose marketing policies until he knows his market*

Experienced exporter Gunnar Beeth offers a pragmatic solution to distributor selection once the market, or a shortlist of markets, has been chosen.[9] It goes like this: first, see the retail buyers and discover which distributors are most successful and respected. Then eliminate those that have obvious conflicts and woo the best of the rest.

Canny as it is, this method will not work in many Asian markets where connections need to be built with retailers before they enter meaningful discussions. These markets usually require more subtlety and persistence. One way or another, personal connections need first to be made based on trust and cultural understanding, both of which take time. Some consultants specialize in this search process, especially in difficult markets such as China. Also, some national embassies are good at assisting this contact process.

Making contacts with potential importers/distributors is probably the single most important key to getting started. It is not just a question of identifying the right importer or distributor, but of convincing them to do business with you. This may not be easy. Because they are successful, they can pick and choose as they wish. Your proposition may at first mean little to them. We advise persistence, consistency, patience. Going with a second choice, an importer/distributor who is over-eager to accept you, may not prove the most profitable long-term relationship. Go with the best. Ideal distributors have outstandingly good relationships with *their* customers, plus a small, highly focussed portfolio which has space for, and is compatible with, your products, and a substantial volume of business or "critical mass."

Critical mass means that the distributor's *portfolio* is big and/or powerful enough to command the attention of (retail) buyers. It is hard to quantify. A highly specialized or prestigious business, for instance, may have critical mass without great volume or market share. If a new product is unique or enjoys special cachet, the attention of distributors can be achieved with modest business volume. The more ordinary the product range, however, the larger the market share needed for critical mass. Market share of 10 percent is a good general rule of thumb (where "market" is understood as immediate customers define it).

Key issues for the importer/distributor are:

- What type of local arrangement is needed for this product category and situation?
- Can you commit for the long term? Can reciprocal trust be established?
- Does the distributor's portfolio fit your products and does it have critical mass?
- How best can you use networking to build relationships with the distributor you want? For example, use prior contacts and market visits.

- How can you ensure the relationship becomes a true partnership? Unequal size is a complication. Small importers do not trust managers in multinationals who job hop regularly and at dizzying speed. Their mistrust is justified. Conversely, small new exporters find it hard to secure already successful, and therefore large, distributors. There is, therefore, a need to assess realistically what each partner is contributing, and for both parties to be comfortable with these contributions.

- Putting differences in national culture aside (these are often more easily identified), how well matched are the *corporate* cultures? Do both partners see the world the same way? Is the way one firm "feels" compatible with the other? The urge to get "married" in the first place should not get in the way of thinking through how the partnership will operate once the honeymoon is over.

Exclusivity has enjoyed popularity, but one should not rule out multiple arrangements. For example, the importer on the US East coast may have no operation on the West coast 3,000 miles away. Most exporters give distributors exclusivity, at least initially, for a simple reason: building brand equity needs time and space. However, don't be surprised if the distributor you approach doesn't want it – there are examples of distributors who are more closely allied with their customers (for example, in specialist sectors such as mining) than their suppliers. They have effectively become outsourced purchasing departments and serve their customers best by having access to a range of suppliers from all over the globe.

A get-to-know phase precedes full commitment. Formal agreements, legal contracts, may be irrelevant. They may even destroy a possibly lasting relationship. Positive attitudes and commitment take time. Agility and interpersonal flexibility cannot operate within legally restrictive language. Empathy needs space and time to breathe. Our interviews with exporters, importers and joint venture partners in the UK, Australia and South East Asia, as well as our personal experience, suggest that gestation periods of between six months and three years are not unusual. Delaying tactics by either side

*Contracts are no way to build business*

are often employed for good reason. On other occasions, overseas partners will sign a piece of paper if it makes the exporter happy. In default, he may help recover some costs, but contracts are no way to build business. Face-to-face time taken up-front by both sides may frustrate head office, but it is more likely to deliver a stronger, smoother business partnership in the long run.

Our research into relationship development is at odds with much of what has been written on market entry. The textbook sequence is to decide the marketing mix and then appoint the distributor. Our research leads us to the opposite view. The *distributor* should normally have the stronger voice in determining the marketing mix and therefore must be appointed first. The reasons include:

- The distributor knows the export market better than the exporter. They live there and have been selected, in part, on their existing performance
- To be motivated and accountable for the results, the distributor must *own* the plan

Both stand to benefit from pooling their skills. Their interests are best served by transferring "knowledge" and becoming "partners" in a particular venture. Not only does the exporter learn and benefit from its partner, but this knowledge brings the network of resources and competencies. One sure sign that a JV (Joint Venture) partnership is strong is the use of "we," when referring to the venture, rather than "them" and "us."

We are not aware of any company that tracks its relationship network formation stages through any formal planning and control systems. While measures are available, firms prefer to leave relationships to intuition, or regard them as given. Different relational dimensions are relevant at different stages. Co-operative behavior is likely to begin in stage two, while trust will start to appear in stage three. A relational audit with key partners can reveal much about the state of play. Managers may feel uncomfortable with developing human relations in that way. Yet much the same applied to manager–subordinate relationships until annual appraisals became standard practice.

Different devices can be employed, or the same devices may be employed differently, depending on the stage of a relationship. Awareness building advertising differs from advertising messages aimed at maintaining and strengthening existing attitudes. Similarly, e-commerce needs to vary with the different stages of the relationship.

Any exporter should be in a learning, not teaching, mode until they understand the new *market*. The distributor likewise must learn about all elements of the *brand* within the context where it has already succeeded. A visit to the home market at the exporter's expense may well be a sound investment, not least to stress commitment. A visit at the distributor's expense can be an even better idea. The distributor immediately has an investment needing a return. In both cases, learning takes place primarily in the relevant country: the foreign market for the exporter and the home market for the importer.

The implications for new market entrants are clear:

- Finding a distributor should not be left to chance, but should involve active networking with those with the strongest potential and interest. Whether through market visits, trade shows or other means, find out where they are and be there

- Commit to your distributor. Work together to plan the marketing program. Co-operation and communication are both positively associated with export performance. More is better

- Audit the relationship annually, perhaps using an experienced independent consultant, as some advertising agencies now do

- Resist the temptation to *control* the new distributor. Clearly one must keep a sharp eye on the cash. But a control orientation is bad for relationship building and implies you know the business better. Actually, they know better than you. Try to *learn* as much as you can, as soon as you can

## Putting people first

The textbook model, in essence, puts analysis first and people last. A small, neophyte exporter is likely to have neither the expertise nor the people to conduct such extensive analysis, nor the resources to engage consultants. Governments signpost information sources and provide basics, subsidize first foreign visits or trade shows, and encourage formal planning. The bank manager probably wants to see the plan too.

A daunting amount of data is available, often more of a barrier than an aid to export. Government agencies believe exporters need more data when really they want less but more insightful information. A supply-driven mentality is stoked by their research. Small and medium enterprises do indeed use information shortage as an excuse when asked why they do not export. The reality is that they do not have time to review what is available. One solution, if the exporter can afford it, is to reduce risk and maximise expertise by buying in specialist resources. Some governments subsidize these services. Consultants' feasibility studies recommend primary markets to enter. Then an external marketing organization can implement the recommendations. Only when the new international business is proven, in this low risk approach, does commitment need to be made to the foreign distributors. An internal exports team can then be recruited.

This "suck it and see" approach is expensive, despite government subsidies, but that is probably not why it is so rare. Successful exporting depends on establishing and committing to long-term *personal* relationships. Personal relationships cannot be thrown around like a football. It is certainly possible for a consultant to set up relationships and then transfer them gradually and sensitively to the firm. Most firms have to learn to do it for themselves.

*Personal relationships cannot be thrown around like a football*

This raises the issue of personnel selection. Bruce Carpenter of Brigham-Young University has identified a number of relational competencies and a competence measurement scale associated with the formation and then the enhancement of personal relationships.[10] These dimensions are:

*Formation* of relationships:

- Assertiveness
- Dominance
- Instrumental competence, i.e. in a particular skill or ability
- Shyness (negatively related)
- Social anxiety (negatively related).

*Enhancement* of relationships:

- Intimacy
- Trust
- Interpersonal sensitivity
- Altruism
- Perspective taking, i.e. empathy.

No doubt this list could be improved and include, for instance, cultural sensitivity.[11] Many firms have quite elaborate criteria for hiring personnel, looking at issues such as problem solving ability, with perhaps one category on "people skills." Such is the importance of relationship formation and development that human resources should research the components of their firm's successful partnerships and use those measurements for recruitment and training. Developing measurement scales to do this is already under way.[12]

# Executive notes

- Relationships are necessary, albeit not sufficient for business success. They may be seen as conduits. We will explore what needs to flow through those conduits in later chapters

- The marketing asset that the firm builds, call it brand equity, reputation or goodwill, consists largely of the sum of these individual relationships

- Components of business relationships, such as trust, commitment, communication, empathy, can be identified and measured, stage by stage. Relationship formation should not be left to chance

- Behavior begets attitudes which in turn beget outcomes, but this is a dynamic model with feedback loops at each stage

- Unequally sized partnerships, for example a small or medium-sized enterprise and multinational corporation, are hard to maintain and easy to sunder. Both partners need critical mass and need to feel comfortable with each other

- In new relationships, e.g. market entry, learning should dominate teaching. Resist the temptation to control
- Whether or not the detailed measures in later chapters are employed, individuals and firms should identify their big business relationships and audit them annually

# References

1. International manager based in Asia – interviewed by one of the authors.
2. The textbooks were: Cateora, P. R. (1993) *International Marketing*. 8th edn. Homewood, Illinois: Irwin; Czinkota, M. R. and Ronkainen, I. A. (1998). *International Marketing*. 5th edn. Fort Worth, TX: The Dryden Press; Terpstra, V. and Sarathy, R. (1997) *International Marketing*. 7th edn. Fort Worth, TX: The Dryden Press; Onkvist, S. and Shaw, J. J. (1990) *International Marketing*. Singapore: Merril Publishing Company; Usunier, J. C. (1993) *International Marketing: A Cultural Approach*. Hemel Hempstead: Prentice Hall; Keegan, W. (1999) *Global Marketing Management*. 6th edn. Upper Saddle River, NJ: Prentice Hall; Bradley, F. *International Marketing Strategy*. 2nd edn. Hemel Hempstead: Prentice Hall.
3. For example, Morgan, R. M. and Hunt, S. D. (1994) "The Commitment-Trust Theory of Relationship Marketing," *Journal of Marketing*, 58 (July), pp. 20–38.
4. Reported in *First Steps to Export Success*, published by the Department of Trade and Industry (UK) and the Australian Trade Commission (1997).
5. Adapted from Styles, C. (1996) *Determinants of Export Performance in Small and Medium Sized Enterprises: An empirical investigation in the UK and Australia*. Unpublished PhD Dissertation, London Business School, p. 62.
6. Based on Dwyer, F. R. *et al.* (1987) "Developing buyer–seller relationships." *Journal of Marketing*, 51 (April), pp. 11–27.
7. For example, Terpstra V. and Sarathy, R. (1991) *International Marketing*, Chapter 10, Dryden International.
Onkvist S. and Shaw, J. (1990) *International Marketing – Analysis and strategy*. Chapter 13. New York: Maxwell Macmillan.
8. Root, F. D. (1987) *Entry Strategies for International Markets*. Lexington, Massachussetts: Lexington Books.
9. Beeth, G. (1991) "Distributors – Finding and Keeping the Good Ones" in Thorelli & Cavusgil (eds), in *International Marketing Strategy*. Oxford: Pergamon Press.
10. Carpenter, B. N. (1993) "Relational Competence" in Perlman, D. and Jones, W. H. (eds) *Advances in Personal Relationships: A research manual*. London: Jessica Kingsley Publishers, pp. 1–28.
11. Phan, M. *et al.* (1999) "A Dyadic Investigation of International Relational Competence Amongst Australian and Malaysian Partnerships." Paper presented at the 12th European Marketing Academy Conference.
12. *See* Phan *et al.* (1999).

# MAC, SILK and PASSION

## An overview

'Nothing was ever achieved without enthusiasm'

*Source:* Ralph Waldo Emerson

---

Relationship marketing draws not only upon our experience in the field but also upon a torrent of thought over the past quarter century that has sought to recapture the body, the emotions, the metaphorical, and the figurative as key drivers of analysis and meaning making. It is this replacement of the mechanical by the natural, or biological, model of business that confirms our experience and provides the main models that underpin this book: MAC, SILK and PASSION.

We first distinguish between the individual manager (MAC) and the firm as a whole (SILK and PASSION). The organizational learning literature regularly slides between the two because it is hard to see how firms adapt and behave except in the way its managers adapt and behave. Yet this distinction is crucial. A firm is not just the sum of its people. It may be more or, in a poorly managed enterprise, less. In our view, the firm should be seen as an organism that exists as independently from its people as we exist independently of our minds and body parts. Of course we cannot exist without them, but at the same time we see ourselves as individuals, not just assemblies.

# MAC

MAC explains how people, be they consumers or managers, make decisions and thus it is also a partial explanation of the whole business generation process.

MAC is derived from modern neuroscience and biology. We have all evolved from, and share more with, other advanced mammals, than differ from them. Rationality and actual knowledge (cognition = C in this model) are as important as Descartes believed them to be for decision making. MAC is post-Cartesian, however, because we now understand it to be only third in line for decision making after our previous experience (memory = M) and our feelings (affect = A).

Clearly, different decisions work in different ways, especially where many people are involved. Nevertheless, *individual* choices are made first on the basis of experience. The great majority are simply habitual (M): our brains are hardly in gear at all. Where the choice is more difficult, we become conscious of it and choice is a matter of feelings (MA). We provide the explanation and justification for this controversial view in Chapter 4. For now, just remind yourself of your last major capital purchase – a house, say, or a car. Most people make the decision very quickly, based on experience and feelings, and then check out the costs and the logic (C). If the cognitive elements fail, they may change their mind or post-rationalize in order to remove the dissonance. So the sequence is M then A then C.

Each provides context for what follows. It is sterile to debate which is more important. An arm is not more important than a leg: each needs to work as well as possible. We should not ignore any one nor confuse their roles; the whole process works together.

We now return from the individual to the organizational level.

# SILK

SILK is the organizational analogue of C at the individual level. We start with this before moving to the more complex PASSION model because information transfer and organizational learning are more familiar territory (due to our Cartesian inheritance, no doubt) than the murky depths of animal spirits and self-identity.

The first step is to recognize that we are not like computers at the individual, nor at the firm, level. Computers communicate digitally: every bit and byte can be counted. We do that with words and numbers – orally, in print, and electronically – but that is only part of our communication, labeled here "explicit." The rest is tacit or implicit and, while we know it works, we do not really know how. Body language and facial expressions have been analyzed and the jury is out on extra-sensory communication.

What we do know, again from biology, is that social information is both important and implicit. Interestingly, the part of our brains that deals with social relationships adjoins the part that houses decision making and feelings.

We justify the model in the next chapter but the key stages are:

1. In the slurry of experiences, data, relationships, and multitudes of impressions that invade our senses, we dimly intuit a value-adding idea. We call this an "outsight" because it is not an under-your-nose obvious thought that everyone has, but something on the periphery of vision.

2. We cannot explicitly share this with anyone because we do not yet know what it is ourselves. We can, however, talk around it with close social contacts who will listen supportively and not knock the idea nor compete. (Social Information = SI).

3. As that process continues, the thought takes shape (it is being "codified") and it is here that its value becomes real, i.e. value is added. (Learning = L).

4. Once it is realized, it can be made explicit and shared across the whole firm.

5. Then it can be implemented.

6. Then others copy, and the value added is eroded by competition.

7. Now two things happen: real Knowledge (K) has been added to the firm's store of intellectual capital and the process will have to start again at 1 above.

The early stage of adding value is a sensitive flower for a simple reason: it has to be different if it is to be better and we instinctively reject other people's differences while enjoying our own neophilia (the love of the new). These, too, are deep-seated biological instincts that we share with other animals. We need to experiment in order to evolve, adapt and survive. On the other hand, if other people step out of line, our hackles rise. We look at "Not Invented

Here," the main obstacle to international marketing, in Chapter 8. Meanwhile, we just need to recognize the need to share these tender shoots only with close associates.

*We need to experiment in order to evolve, adapt and survive*

Taking the whole circuit, SI leads to L which in turn leads to organizational knowledge (K). Many of the world's largest firms are now taking this area seriously enough to appoint chief knowledge officers with sweeping powers to gather together their firm's processes and databases.

## PASSION

The "SION" (Social Information and Organizational kNowledge) is the same as SILK and is renamed only for the acronym and because SION has other meanings. Just as in the MAC model, cognition comes last so, for the organization, does SILK. We give priority to corporate Purpose (and identity) – P – and then to the energizing life force itself, which Descartes, and then Maynard Keynes, termed "animal spirits" – AS.

Once again, and paradoxically you may think, we do not regard any one as the driver of the others, nor is one more important than the others. If you like metaphors, consider a car. Purpose provides direction (the steering wheel = P), the engine provides energy and power (animal spirits = AS) and the electronic systems and connections provide the in-built cognition (SION). Modern cars have on-board computers which adapt to environment and drivers. It makes no sense to say the steering is more important than the engine: they all have to work together (synergize) for the car to work at all.

In seeking to restore the body to the mind and the spirit to the flesh, relationship marketing calls upon new conceptual models that not only incorporate, but also give salience to the natural, the biological. This is in distinction to the main classical model of business: the economic.

# What international managers do
## Networks of SILK

'We are all Adam's children but silk makes the difference'
*Source:* T. Fuller[1]

'Learning has replaced control as the fundamental job of the manager'
*Source:* S. Zuboff[2]

## United Biscuits – international trading development manager

Reporting to the international sales development controller, you will have responsibility for developing markets within Asia and Central and Eastern Europe. You will in effect act as an international sales consultant and be charged with introducing the required processes and skills to enhance operational efficiency and effectiveness in conjunction with the development of sales in these markets.

This is a demanding role with high visible impact on the company's success and will involve considerable and lengthy travelling. You must demonstrate a strong capacity for flexibility and have the credibility to operate across these very challenging markets.

*Source:* job advertisement in *The Times*, 15 January 1998

International marketers roam across national and functional borders in order to create wealth for the firm through learning and adaptation. In many respects, they provide the adhesive of social information and motivation, spreading a sense of corporate identity and purpose across wide networks. The United Biscuits job advertisement as consultant and trainer is no special case: all international marketers are consultants and trainers. Why else would they sometimes travel 14 hours at great social, health, and economic cost for a one-hour meeting? Simply for information which could be sent electronically?

Today information can be transmitted, processed, and analyzed, decisions can be made, communicated and implemented – all without anyone leaving the office. As processing and analysis become automated and communications tools more sophisticated, the need for face-to-face meetings should reduce. Managers could stay at home, compute, and avoid all that expense and hassle. In fact, air passenger statistics show ever increasing business travel. Why in this day and age do so many intelligent people spend so much time hurtling around the planet?

The answer goes to the heart of how business makes money: changing behavior results from sharing social information. Profits and shareholder value arises from the way information is created, shared, and transmitted between individuals engaged in common purpose.

*Creative people with imagination need to be roaming the frontiers and stalking the jungles in search of the unexpected, the unpredictable*

Managers travel in order to create social networks and to capture experiences that cannot be understood in purely objective terms. In all fields, creative people with imagination need to be roaming the frontiers and stalking the jungles in search of the unexpected, the unpredictable. They scan and test; they find patterns that others miss; they notice business opportunities in the visual periphery that lack articulation and definition; they come away with a notion, a concept, a fresh idea. One sight, as the Chinese say, is worth a thousand sayings, especially when the sight is something others have missed. We are not dealing with the tunnel vision of formal planning, but vague images, perceptions out on the edge.

Then begins the long process of teasing that notion into something of value. Most, perhaps all, great commercial ideas emerge in this manner. The sparks of ideas that led to diet foods, trainers, PCs, and the Walkman, arrived from outside the mainstream of familiar analytical data. To squeeze the travel budget may be false economy. In the disastrous launch of Cleopatra soap in

Canada in the 1980s, the outcome might have been very different had the Canadians visited France to study the brand's success there.[3] As it was, the Canadians, with no personal experience of the French success, were unconvinced by the opportunity and committed a series of marketing *faux pas* with predictable lack of success.

The personal relationship is the fundamental dyad of business, but it is only a conduit. It makes value creation possible but does not drive creativity. Great relationships do not necessarily lead to great business. The value of these relationships lies in providing the channels first for exchanging implicit, experiential information. These channels also carry explicit (verbal and digital) information and, as we will see in Chapter 6, the enthusiasm and energy that really drive the organization. In this chapter, we consider how a firm's learning and knowledge builds up from these dyadic relationships.

*The personal relationship is the fundamental dyad of business*

We call the cycle of value creation the Social Information → Learning → Knowledge, or SILK, process. SILK is the path by which the organization translates implicit, local, and transient information into permanent knowledge shared by the whole firm. And knowledge, let us agree, is crucial for the firm's fundamental competitive advantage.

## The SILK model of international marketing

Theories of information, such as those of Ikujiro Nonaka and Hirotaka Takeuchi, and ESADE's Professor Max Boisot, suggest that competitive advantage and wealth creation arise from the firm's process of sharing experiential information through social interaction and its subsequent conversion to explicit information.[4] In these theories, innovation is given salience, and innovation is precisely what micro-economics, given its orientation toward static equilibrium, has been unable to explain.

Standing on the shoulders of Boisot *et al.*, the SILK model portrays international marketing as value creation for the firm through purposive organizational learning, basically as that learning fosters the innovative process of translating vague notions into explicit information that can be implemented.

This may seem somewhat loose and subjective, but our own research indicates that formal or objective information processing, however important, is secondary because it is the mechanical part of understanding and post-hoc rationalizing of creative solutions. Firms check out the mathematics before they put the solutions in hand. But the mathematics do not create the solutions. Objective analysis needs to follow, not precede, the sharing of experiential information. This idea stands in contrast to the neoclassical, or Cartesian, model in which rational analysis of objective information gives no attention to the crucial, creative precursors. The Cartesian framework is primarily financial. "Anything worth considering can be counted" overstates this approach, but not by much. SILK, by contrast, recognizes observed practice where learning takes place *before* information can be expressed quantitatively, i.e. "counting can be left until we have to justify the decision." This does not mean decisions should be made in a blind, shooting-from-the-hip manner. Rather, we are recognizing that the processes managers *really* use to make (versus justify) decisions is far deeper than what can be expressed on a spreadsheet.

## Wine buying

Travel hasn't always been seen as necessary or beneficial for international trade. Traditional London wine merchants used to counsel against visiting vineyards. Judgment, they said, was warped by local experience. There was sense in this. Wine lovers everywhere know that the wine that tasted so delicious in the sunny South of France suffers when quaffed on a wet winter Wednesday in Wigan. The wine merchant who stays at home can better identify with the palates of his customers. If the urge to travel became overwhelming, they advised, make no decision until the samples arrive back in the office. Conversely, the wine makers wanted buyers to visit precisely because that was where the wines showed best.

Wine, of course, is more sensitive to its environment than, say, machine tools. As such it may be a special case but the story has a moral: why is that old advice now routinely ignored? The exporter and the importer need never meet, and yet they do.

## Implicit information and value creation

Edith Penrose distinguished two types of knowledge.[5] The first, objective (or explicit) knowledge, can be formally taught and transmitted through books, reports, spreadsheets, and such. The second, implicit (or experiential) knowledge, comes from the personal, unstructured joys and woes of individual living and is transmitted (although never completely) through artistic expression and the interpersonal non-verbal communications we all experience, even though we do not understand how they work.

The difficulty of converting experiential (the implicit or tacit) into objective (explicit) information explains why we must interact with others. We cannot leave new ideas to computers or formal systems; they lack agility, and imagination and the ability to make creative connections between nodes of information in the same way that the human mind can. International business people, marketers especially, cross-fertilize information of all sorts between the parts of their own organization and outsiders. In the wine buying example, we see that traders must meet and get to know each other to gain real knowledge about the wine and each other. You could, and some do, buy and sell anonymous parcels, perhaps at auction. But most of the trade relies on each stage of the distribution chain developing personal trust. At the supermarket stage, a "parasocial" relationship between the retail brand and consumer takes over to provide equivalent reassurance.

Figure 3.1 shows the value creation cycle. We begin at the bottom right-hand corner. Earlier ideas have dissipated whatever profit potential they had and we are looking for something new. At the "outsights" stage (arrow A) images from the world about us are scattered higgledy piggledy; there are so many fleeting and vague concepts. Some are obvious everyone else sees them too and we reject them as boring. Maybe one or two others, not many, seem potentially valuable. The arrow signifies that we are drawing, from a mass of information available to everyone, a new personal outsights – a unique pattern that emerges from chaos.

*An apparently empty space may be a Bermuda triangle of previous disasters or a fresh opportunity*

Environmental scanning shows a scattered range of products, markets, prices and qualities. An apparently empty space may be a Bermuda triangle of previous disasters or a fresh opportunity. Conversely, a busy market may

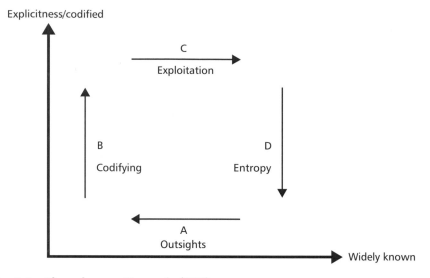

**Fig. 3.1    The value creation cycle (SILK)**

be overloaded or the place where the action is. Popularity proves nothing. New ideas and "outsights" are needed. The word "outsight" is coined to imply it is:

1. External, i.e. from the environment

2. Peripheral

3. Lateral, and not linear.

It stands as a counterpart to tunnel vision and insight.

Successful entrepreneurs are gifted with more outsight capacity than their intellectual equals, as well as with a greater ability to communicate these outsights to their immediate team. Showing large and complex pictures to entrepreneurs and non-entrepreneurs, matched in other respects, resulted in the first group seeing more in the picture, especially round the perimeter, and communicating better what they saw.

At the origin of Figure 3.1 (bottom left) we can socially communicate some aspects of these notions to a few close colleagues. In business we share sensitive ideas, and humor, with some colleagues but not others. As the notions begin to form, some will be rejected as impractical, but perhaps one will begin to look more attractive as it takes shape. The process of rendering an implicit notion explicit, of converting a vague idea into an implementable solution, may be called problem solving or codifying. In Figure 3.1 it is represented by arrow B.

We used to believe in the "hopper" or "shotgun" approach to new product development – many firms still do. This generates many ideas, through brainstorming or agencies, which are progressively reduced through analysis and market research to one or a few survivors, which are then developed and launched. The process has had limited success. The alternative "rifle" approach, which usually works better (there are no guarantees in the new product business), gives early focus to one really great idea (as distinct from a mass of dubious ideas) and then uses a process analogous to Figure 3.1 to hone, refine and revise it until its chances are maximized. Totally committed to that one concept, just as one is committed to an only child, we do whatever we can to make it successful.

One has little choice but to allow the untidy and a-rational cycle to reveal its answers in its own slow, shape-shifting manner. We have all experienced unformed ideas that, no matter how we cudgel our brains or each other, do not solve the problems we want solved. Suddenly, after a night's sleep, all the pieces fit together with little conscious effort. A coherent plan emerges. We do not know how this happens, but we know it does.

Near the top of arrow B, analytic processes and market research will be brought to bear. If the innovation cannot withstand that attack, it should either be dropped or, more likely, sent back for revision. In any case, arrow B represents the vital, value-creating stage. Once at the top it can be implemented. Arrow C is the mass introduction stage where the value created can be harvested.

If our portrait of SILK implies the complete rejection of quantitative analysis, we have given the wrong impression. Measurement is important but it follows and can reverse decision making. We decide we want to buy a condominium, for example, before we calculate and commit to paying for it. Research into strategic decision making by large, sophisticated firms has found the same phenomenon: analysis is necessary, but secondary.

This idea, that the conversion of implicit to explicit is the core generator of business profits, may explain why Eastern firms are so reluctant to share core experience and why they regard Western openness as naive. Keeping marketing process, not just facts, confidential is not limited to the East. Procter & Gamble and Mars prohibit staff discussing marketing matters with media or outsiders. The SILK model requires organizational learning to be shared with insiders, not outsiders.

With any new marketing innovation, success will bring competition and margins will be put under pressure. This is usually, but erroneously, called the brand life cycle. Brands do not have life cycles. Their managers do and some cause the death of their brands through bad marketing, notably the failure to innovate the underlying products when necessary. Withering margins result not from "mature market conditions" (refer to numerous brand manager/CEO presentations), but the failure of management to move the brand and lead the category into the next stage of innovation – margins don't happen to managers, managers create the opportunity for margins. The underlying products do not necessarily have life cycles either, though this is less of a wrong analogy. Products die when better ones take their place. If no better product can be found, e.g. salt, then the product lives forever.

Nevertheless, for whatever reason, the marketing innovation will run out of steam and entropy will set in. It will lose its rationale. This is signified by arrow D that takes us back to the beginning of the cycle. We now need to relate that value creation cycle to SILK.

The conversion of social information to organizational learning (SI → L) is also represented by arrow B. That obviously uses whatever knowledge the firm has during the problem-solving or codifying stage. Conversely, the learning outputs from all stages (arrows A–D) feed into the organizational knowledge (L → K).

This is a form of "double loop learning," where the higher level loop (knowledge) influences the *way* the lower loop in Figure 3.1 operates. For example, new understanding changes behavior, which in the past has led to wrong choices. This carries us back to the thrust of experiential social information being toward changed behavior. However, this is never easy. Individuals and organizations are highly resistant to changing behavior. While organizations can only learn through their individual members, organizations also create systemic constraints that prevent their individual members from learning and sharing that learning. The wary international marketer must read the rhythm and understand this resistance.

Differential advantage, and thereby wealth potential, lies with those who have developed the higher loop level (knowledge and systems) that governs the value creation cycle, relative to those who have not. The problem and its solution cannot be codified, i.e. put into language the rest of the firm can handle, without being part of the social group.

The thesis that value arises from the conversion of implicit to explicit information, that, in effect, nature acts informationally as well as energetically, carries major implications for wealth generation. Boisot, as well as Nonaka and Takeuchi, provides compelling anecdotal and theoretical evidence. Our own research in overseas market entry bears it out. Exporters rated experiential data collection (e.g. personal discussions with distributors and market visits) more highly, in terms of usefulness for decision making, than objective data collection (e.g., published data, formal market research).[6] Business school graduates find it hard to accept, but the managers have got it right. In our research, experiential data collection was positively correlated with performance, while no significant relationship existed between objective data collection and performance.

## Organizational learning

'In the simplest sense, a learning organization is a group of people who are continually enhancing their capability to create their future'[7]

As an experiential learning cycle, does SILK play by the same rules as organizational learning theory in general? George Washington University's Professor Nancy Dixon reviews 11 definitions of organizational learning and finds four common themes – all are shared by the SILK model.[8]

- The expectation that increased *knowledge* will improve action.
- An acknowledgement of the pivotal *relationship* between the organization and the environment. That the environment is the major element that the organization must learn and to which the organization must adapt or manipulate.
- The idea of solidarity, as in collective or *shared thinking*, that members of an organization have shared assumptions in common, which may need to be uncovered, corrected, or expanded to facilitate effective organizational action.
- A proactive stance in terms of *the organization changing itself.* Many definitions imply that, through learning, the organization is able to

self-correct in response to environmental change or to transform itself in anticipation of a desired future.

In other words:

- First, the personal relationships, the dyads, between managers in the firm and business partners outside, must be constructed. These are the conduits through which information (and more, as will be discussed later) will flow.

- Second, the lower level loop of SILK uses those relationships to create value.

- Third, the progressive circuits of SILK build knowledge and a culture, which facilitate new relationships and more value-creating loops.

In other words, this is a virtuous double loop of organizational learning.

Identifying a firm's core competence(s), or distinctive capabilities, and basing new product development on that capability, became a popular sport for late twentieth century strategists and human relations executives.[8] It was a sign of the times that strategy had started focussing on the softer issues. The one-time preoccupation with competition (War) and control was replaced by a concern for empowerment and innovation. Directionally it was probably right but, like postmodernism, it rejected narrow rationality without any underlying scientific discipline. The fashionable business language of competence and values is in the ballpark but lacks substance. We can all retro-fit competence to explain success *after* it has happened, but what managers really need to know is how to create value in the first place. We need to predict.

*No one person owns the truth. Knowledge lies between people rather than within their heads*

The SILK model anchors these beliefs in social psychology, human experience, and relationships. Shared values are indeed necessary for social, implicit information to spark wealth creation but, like relationships, they are not enough.

We suggest:

- That each firm develop its own distinctive capability that causes it to grow or diminish relative to competition. This is the third stage above and requires measurement.

- Creating a system to identify opportunities others miss (arrow A in Figure 3.1). One of the factors that caused General Electric to throw out their 1970s planning system was its tunnel vision: its focus on existing activities caused them to miss the "white space" outside.

- That the marketer foster open dialogue and a confrontation of conflicts. No one person owns the truth. Knowledge lies between people rather than within their heads. Imagine managers as neurons in the corporate brain. Just as a single memory component in our brain is a synapse joining two neurons, our knowledge is built from interpersonal connections.

- Corporate knowledge is a "black box": good learning goes in and we can identify consequential benefits. In between, we do not need to spend much time identifying the precise contents of the box. We know that the key elements are implicit. By the time it solidifies and becomes explicit, like lava, its force is largely spent.

- Not worrying about the state of the knowledge (or capabilities) themselves but creating three stages of *process* that build them.

In effect, the SILK model portrays international marketing as enabling the firm to learn. Since the model deals with the firm as a whole it does not address internal differences. It assumes positive, constructive relationships between managers when, in practice, there may exist many obstacles to learning and sharing. What its managers see as good for the local business unit may not be good for the firm as a whole. Measurement, discussed later, goes a long way to harmonize purpose and remove learning blockages.

## On the SILK road: weaving between and within markets

While spreading webs of silk is central to the work of international marketers, their work is by no means only informational. Other roles include:

- *Coach.* Shows how higher performance is feasible and how others have achieved it. The coach takes the initiative in providing relevant information but, more importantly, in encouraging the motivation to learn.

- *Consultant.* Provides similar information, but here the initiative lies with the local business to use the service to determine feasible solutions to their trading issues.

- *Partner.* The local unit is responsible for its own results but, in most global businesses, the international marketer is accountable too.

- *Member of the planning team.* Fully involved as distinct from being an outsider.

- *Controller.* Ensuring that performance meets expectations. We stress the positive aspects of SILK but policing, however discreetly, is a practical necessity.

A promotion from national to international marketer is a quantum leap in role and responsibility, basically from player to coach. One cannot simply switch successful national experience to the international. Entire new dimensions of systems and network understanding are involved. Unless the firm has "gone global" and treats the world as a single entity with no national boundaries (which is quite rare), the international marketing manager must understand an unwieldy assembly of markets, each unique, and then show the restraint to apply that understanding indirectly through social information. Just applying his previous national experience is most likely to alienate the new nationals.

What the international marketer does *not* do is to market. He or she operates *between* (national) markets and not, generally, *within* them.

The normal reaction of national marketers is to dismiss foreign experience as irrelevant to local needs and to reject ideas from abroad because they are not invented here (NIH). Here is one of those obstacles to learning and value creation that the marketer must understand and overcome.

*The international marketer is both coach and student of the national marketer*

Most companies, if they warrant the name "international" at all, share authority across a hierarchy of local, national, regional and global responsibilities. They involve some form of matrix organization, however they might resist the term. Where national firms have separate marketing departments, they report to national chief executives. The international marketer, as part of regional or global HQ, typically has responsibility without power.

In essence, the international marketer is both coach and student of the national marketer. He is coach because he brings knowledge – from the past and from other markets – and motivation. He is student because he learns from local experience. This cross-fertilization can take many forms, two of which come from biology.

## Two role models: butterfly and bee

The SILK metaphor probably suggests moths whose dictionary definition (Chambers 1993) includes "a fragile, frivolous creature, readily dazzled into destruction." Like workaholic international managers, moths tend to travel by night. Nevertheless, it is butterflies and bees that characterize the two better approaches to cross-fertilization.

In the worker bee model, the international marketing centre – the hive – is the repository of knowledge. International marketers travel in order to bring back information, in the broad sense. The butterfly, however, cross-fertilizes directly between national units: the centre has no significance. The butterfly makes no individual contribution, while the bee is part of the team and the honey-making process. The butterfly travels to enjoy life and accidentally cross-pollinates as it goes. Each works well in the right structural context and badly in others. The SILK model applies to both; the issue is whether the national units are largely autonomous or centrally co-ordinated.

Whether the national units are affiliates within a global group, or independent partners, (e.g. JV, distributor or licensee) matters little to the international brand manager. The role is much the same: coaching and learning, with some elements of control. Nevertheless, the internal politics of a multinational can frustrate the visitor. Local units complain of interference and point out that they are the ones making the money. The benefits of cross-fertilization for *future* profits are less obvious to local marketers preoccupied by fire fighting.

A single site unit shares information naturally. Boundaries, be they between functions, business units or countries, complicate the picture. Not everything can be shared, nor can units be hermetically sealed and remain part of a wider organization in any real sense. The subsidiary may consider too much time is wasted in supplying information to the center at the same time as the center believes the information to be inadequate. The border has become an impediment: the center and the subsidiaries are *competing* for scarce resources. In this scenario, the center may not be adding value.

Assuming the international manager has the locals' affection and attention, which pollinating role should he adopt? In butterfly mode, the visitor learns from the successes and failures of the local team and then shares relevant experiences from elsewhere. He does not become involved nor express strong opinions of his own. On returning to base, he does much the same. In worker bee mode, he becomes an active member of the local, regional and global planning teams. Which works better depends on the personalities and corporate cultures involved. Of course the biological metaphor is not exact.

In the 1990s, the "transnational" restructuring of British Petroleum aimed to cross-fertilize rather than disseminate learning from global headquarters. In this way it sought to hollow out the center and move from bee to butterfly mode.

A swarm of bees demonstrates more intelligence (learning) as a whole than any sub-group or any individual. Unlike butterflies, the bees are organized as a team. Their "consciousness" is collective because they are genetically identical. Managers, no matter how long they have rubbed along, remain genetically distinct. As Arie de Geus has pointed out, the social congregation is both significant and important.[9] Tits flock together and adapt rapidly to environmental changes, such as to the introduction of foil milk bottle tops. They quickly learned to peck through to reach the cream and within a few weeks the whole flock had learned. Robins, however, are antisocial and learn very little. They still cannot reach the cream. Large organizations remain effective in the world market-place, even when large numbers of staff come and go, provided the culture promotes social information sharing.

*A swarm of bees demonstrates more intelligence [learning] as a whole than any sub-group or any individual*

When GrandMet acquired Pillsbury, for example, virtually the entire Minneapolis executive cadre was replaced by newcomers from other companies and other US/European locations. Nevertheless, the Pillsbury culture was not greatly altered. People suggested that the physical characteristics of the HQ might be a reason. In other words, if you want to change the culture, change the hive.

In summary, international marketers can be seen as the connectors within the corporate whole. They network in such a way that social information, learning and knowledge can be shared. That, in turn, makes objective information, whose importance we do not denigrate, easier to exchange and assimilate. Their style may be butterfly, bee, police officer, or some combination, depending on context. The same individual may elect to be policeman (pure controller) in Russia, butterfly in the US and bee in Japan.

# Executive notes

This chapter has made the following points:

- An organization is an organism. Whether it lives, dies or merely survives depends on the extent to which it is able to convert social information → learning → knowledge

- Objective (explicit) information differs from experiential (implicit or tacit)

- Growing the business, wealth creation, requires the sharing and conversion of experiential into explicit information, which drives profit until the information becomes commonplace and entropy takes over

- The process has three stages: creating the network of dyadic relationships, the conduits; the value-creating SILK cycle, and the higher-level knowledge and culture building that facilitates the first two

- SILK can be seen as interpersonal connections within the corporate mind

- Within this SILK culture, the international marketer should be a coach, not a player. He or she is also consultant, partner, part of the planning team (double loop learning), and low-key controller (single loop learning)

- International marketers connect and cross-fertilize experiential information as working members of teams (bee) and/or in less involved modes (butterfly)

# References

1. Fuller, T. (1732) *Gnomologia*, #5425.
2. Zuboff, S. (1989) *In the Age of the Smart Machine: The future of work and power*. Reprint edition. New York: Basic Books.
3. *Source*: HBS case study.
4. Boisot, M. (1995) *Information Space*. London: Routledge.
   Nonaka, I. and Takeuchi, H. (1995) *The Knowledge-Creating Company*. Oxford: Oxford University Press.
5. Penrose, E. (1966) *The Theory of the Growth of the Firm*. Oxford: Basil Blackwell.
6. Styles C. and Ambler, T. (1997) *First Steps to Export Success*, pp. 7 & 8. Australian Trade Commission and The Department of Trade and Industry (UK), January. Also, Styles, C. (1996) PhD Dissertation, London Business School, pp. 31, 60 & 61.
7. Quoted in Napuk K. (1994) "Live and learn," *Scottish Insider*, January.
8. Dixon, N. (1999) *The Organizational Learning Cycle*, 2nd Edition. New York: McGraw-Hill.
9. de Geus, A. (1997) *The Living Company*. London: Nicholas Brealey p. 162.

chapter

# 4

## MAC

## How marketing decisions are made

'History advances in disguise; it appears on stage wearing the mask of the preceding scene, and we tend to lose the meaning of the play. The blame, of course, is not history's, but lies in our vision, encumbered with memory and images learned in the past. We see the past superimposed on the present, even when the present is a revolution.'

*Source:* R. Debray[1]

'Walk abroad and recreate yourselves'

*Source:* William Shakespeare[2]

Hossegor, on France's Atlantic Coast, doesn't quite conjure up the same image as Sydney's Bondi Beach. But both have one thing in common — surfers wearing boardshorts and T-shirts sporting the Quicksilver brand. It was not always so, and perhaps should not have been so, if we believe what the textbooks tell us.

It all began on a snowy January day in 1984, when the newly appointed heads of Australian surf brand Quicksilver's European division were struggling to make their first trade show in Paris. Somewhere en route, their foam stall was blown off the roof of their old Citroën. As Jeff Hakman, a former world surfing Champion, pinned up the company's bright boardshorts on the bare walls, he looked at his business partner, Harry Hodge, then at the snow outside and their summery singlets. "I don't think this is going to work," he said. But gradually it did. Quicksilver Europe now makes around five times the annual profit of the founding Australian company.

What was the key to their success? Market analysis, a strategic plan, and adequate financial backing? Not quite. They openly admit that their European start-up was ridiculously under-financed, with Hodge and his team having to beg their bank manager to lend them money every Friday to pay their seamstress. But Hodge remained optimistic, and his observations while attending another trade show – this time a windsurfing show in Germany – gives us insight as to why. "I walked around the show and there were all these fat 50-year-olds in suits, drinking whisky and smoking cigars. They had no passion to live the lifestyle. And I said to Jeff, 'This is going to be easy. We might be young and naive, but at least we do the sports and we can smell the industry.'"

This passion eventually translated into the development of a whole new range of clothing, mountain gear, which came to Hodge as he slalomed down the Alpine slopes amongst scores of young snowboarders. Explains Hodge, "It's the same spirit as the ocean. Probably because of the passion we developed for the mountains, we were able to make clothes that corresponded with what the kids wanted." He may not have had much hard data to go on, but he had a feeling it would work.

Adapted from "Chairman of the boardies," by Sarah Turnbull, *The Australian Magazine*, 7–8 August 1999, pp. 24–28

---

If the old, mechanical ideals of business strategy are falling into disrepute, what replaces pure cognitive processes in showing us how to build brand equity?

What we find is quite appealing. We find the entire human sensing apparatus eager for participation. We find memory, personal history, value judgements, experiences, relationships, empathy; in fact, our entire affective lives. Each plays an important role in human choice behavior, whether those humans are international marketers or grocery shoppers.

The task before us, in understanding marketing decisions, is not to throw out the old in favor of the sparkling new, but to find the synthesis and interplay between sensing and thinking, between the affective and the cognitive. To build a brand–customer relationship, marketing needs to understand what factors lie at the heart of choices. That includes empathy with the customer. Marketers are less concerned with how people should be, or how their decisions should be made, as described by an economic model, than by how they really are.

It is not obvious, and may not be true, that as consumers we make decisions in a different way than we make decisions as marketers. In fact, we use the same mental apparatus. All decisions are based on new information inputs, memories, and experience. Marketers are also consumers. Clearly, different decisions are made in different ways. The care given to buying a new home is quite different from choosing a loaf of bread. Nevertheless, marketing decisions made by sellers do not essentially differ from those made by buyers.

We will build a model, from research, for how *all* marketing decisions are made and how they need to be seen in social context. In so doing, we bring Memory, Affect (feeling), as well as Cognition (thinking), into mutual support. This we call the MAC model of decision making, which includes a feedback loop from customer experience. *See* Figure 4.1, overleaf.

Relating to individuals in many different markets, experiencing the uniqueness of their cultures and concerns, certainly helps, but more is required. Seeing through differences to similarities enables learning to transfer between markets. The barriers created by our own minds are far more crucial than those arising from national borders.

So, let us first examine a few important characteristics of the human mind that determine choices and decisions, aside from logical reasoning. A "mental model" is a simplified version of reality that we use to test the consequences of what we do.

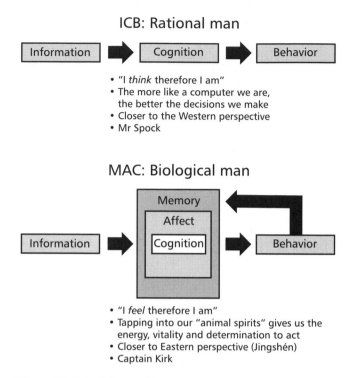

## ICB: Rational man

| Information | ➡ | Cognition | ➡ | Behavior |

- "I *think* therefore I am"
- The more like a computer we are, the better the decisions we make
- Closer to the Western perspective
- Mr Spock

## MAC: Biological man

- "I *feel* therefore I am"
- Tapping into our "animal spirits" gives us the energy, vitality and determination to act
- Closer to Eastern perspective (Jīngshén)
- Captain Kirk

**Fig. 4.1   ICB vs. MAC decision making**

# Mental models

Mental models have a major impact on the way we make decisions. These models consist of a random blend of fact and fiction, stories and experience, the received, unquestioned wisdom of a particular culture. These models indicate certain paths and options: some will seem desirable and make sense while others will not. Just as a toy train is a long way from being a train, any mental model will be far short of reality. Their value depends on context. The toy train is fine for six year olds but not for training engine drivers.

In many ways models act as perceptual filters. To deal with the hourly, daily bombardment of data, emotions, noises, accidents, e-mails, phone calls, etc., we channel information, we filter and we screen out the irrelevant. If we didn't, we'd go crazy. So we simplify the way we see things. But quite often these filters and screens blind us. They may cause us to stereotype, to narrow our perceptions. They lead to the automatic and the reflexive, rather than the unique. In the field of international marketing, the "virtual reality helmet" of national culture distorts what we observe.

## Ethnocentricity

Roger Adams was vice-president, marketing, for the US business of a global oil company in the 1970s. In that turbulent decade he was outstandingly successful and when the world-wide marketing presidency fell vacant, Roger was the unanimous choice. In his new role, he struggled. National marketers rejected the insights he brought and world-wide promotions never got off the ground. Standardized planning systems proved unpopular and failed to anticipate competitor successes. There was continual wrangling over who would direct, and pay for, market research. Some were unkind enough to suggest that, previously, he had just been lucky.

Roger's case is not unique. The same story could be told of many promising executives promoted from national to international responsibilities. Their employers failed to recognize that the role of an international marketing executive is not the same as that of his national marketing counterpart. It bears repeating: the job of an *inter*national marketer is working *between* national markets. That is, after all, what "inter" means.

It's a problem common to all walks of life. Each one of us lives within a set of assumptions about the world that we use to make sense of any new environment or job. It was natural for Roger Adams to approach his new role as an extension of what he was doing before. Since his past practices had clearly worked, why change them? After all, why was he promoted? This inability to "think outside the box," so to speak, continues to confound international marketers everywhere.

Roger Adams wore a "virtual reality helmet" constructed from three elements:

- *National culture.* He instinctively knew how US marketers and customers would respond to his proposals. He could evaluate marketing plans quickly and accurately. Judgment, they say, is the result of bad experiences and Roger had had his fair share. Now, however, he *knew* what was right without having to think about it and, more significantly, without being *able* to think about it.

- *Personal history.* He saw things in the way he had been trained to see them. The marketing he learned at business school required solid market research, analysis, and segmentation. Then you cranked the numbers to determine and allocate the marketing budget, and the marketing plan fell out. This approach was simply not appropriate to his new role.

- *Rational analysis.* For Roger, decision making was a matter of logic, statistics and probabilities. The end users may seem irrational – emotional even – but ultimately they are maximising their utilities. Business decisions are driven by optimising shareholder value and, if they are not, then they damn well should be.

Let us sympathize with Roger. Our perceptions are strongly influenced by how we have been trained. The economist, the psychologist, and the military general will describe the same events in quite different ways. In consequence, they will take different actions. This is why successful marketers find it so difficult to transfer their skills from one sector to another. Intuition arises from experience which, in the new environment, is fallible.

According to a historian of the Cuban revolution, Regis Debray, we make sense of the world by imposing our own history on it. Yet the fundamental message of marketing is to see the business from the *consumer's* point of view. The problem for the new international marketer is that the more foreign the consumer, the less reliable his own personal instincts and experience.

> *The fundamental message of marketing is to see the business from the consumer's point of view*

Bertrand Collomb holds a PhD from the University of Texas and ran France's La-Farge Coppée, the world's second-largest cement maker. Recognizing the slant that national culture places on understanding, he observed: "You need to take people out of their original culture because once you do that you open them to everything else."[3] A colleague recently took a group of senior executives from a European auto firm to Vietnam, originally to consider market entry into that part of Asia. As it turned out, market entry took a back seat to debating how their own firm was being managed. Taking the executives out of their usual environment helped them see themselves with greater clarity.

Thus our ways of thinking arise both from the culture(s) in which we grow up and the education and training we receive. Some believe that childhood exposure to foreign cultures is essential for expatriates and international marketers, but understanding cultural differences is not enough; international marketers must adapt to them, and adaptation becomes more difficult as an adult, especially when the single culture has been reinforced by success over many years.

Delayed in leaving the head office, Roger got off the plane in Frankfurt tired and rushed. He found the German company team had developed the annual marketing plan, based on their shared experiences and past successes and failures. They had taken their plan through a few rounds of challenge within their own business. Some, but only some, of this appeared in the written plan. In any case, the discussion had been in German, but the plan had to be in English. Topics not challenged or changed – the strategy, for example – were not included at all. The budget was there and so was the investment that would be required to support the promotional activity to reverse recent losses of market share.

Roger saw those promotions as simple price discounts, which would prove ineffective if matched by the competition. At best they were expensive and would damage the reputation of the brand. He had not, however, come simply to sign off the German budget. He wanted to share new global market research and tell them about successes in other markets. The Germans just wanted their plan approved and some central subsidy to help their competitive problems. They believed that if these were not addressed in Germany, they would spread to the rest of Europe. They let Roger know they were not interested in market research from other countries, even those next door.

Similar encounters between international and national marketers are common. For the moment, Roger's lesson from his German trip is that he is no longer a national marketer himself, but an executive charged with the task of motivating better performance from the nationals. As the story begins, he is ineffective. He needs to make a conscious effort to first build a relationship with the German team. He is neither butterfly nor bee because he is not part of the German firm's social group.

But, like many managers, Roger is a prisoner of his business school training as well as his earlier career. To understand what he – and many like him – are up against, we must take a step back and look at the evolution of what we mean by "relationship marketing."

## Marketing paradigms

Few business people have any difficulty in recalling that marketing means satisfying customers at a profit, or words to that effect. In practice it is not so simple. Which customers? Trade buyers or end users? Does "marketing" involve the whole company or just the marketing department? If the whole company, how is "marketing" different from "business"? Those who see themselves as marketers naturally enough see marketing as a whole company activity directed by themselves. Those managing other functions will see marketing more narrowly. They will see their own role, speciality, or division – not marketing – as central to total corporate performance. Again, we are dealing with virtual reality helmets.

Clearly, marketing cannot be not fully represented by the annual plan. To keep it brief and focused, much has to be implicit. A plan depends on what it is *for*. Many are designed to gain support for the proposed marketing expenditure. Following the Canadian humorist Stephen Leacock, a marketing plan has been described as a device for arresting the intelligence of the chief financial officer long enough to take money off him.

As we noted in the introduction, marketing paradigms evolved sequentially from the original "neoclassical" (or Math) to competitive strategy (or War) to relationships (love or Empathy). In the first of these, firms calculated what mix of marketing activities (the 4Ps – Product, Pricing, Promotion and Place) yielded the best profit return. In the second, firms considered how to gain differential advantage over competitors. As in any war, short-term costs were subordinate to destroying the enemy. In the final paradigm, end user satisfaction is reinstated as the primary objective. Professor Philip Kotler, author of the leading neoclassical textbook, now sees the marketplace as a "network of value-laden relationships."[4] His ninth edition states that, "transaction marketing" (neoclassical) is "part of a larger idea called relationship marketing."[5]

The second view of marketing, War, became popular in the late 1960s and 1970s. That period saw a growing interest in market share as the key determinant of business success. PIMS, a Cambridge-based econometric spin-off from General Electric and Harvard Business School, created a pooled database and deduced that market share, or market rank, drove profitability.

In other words, profitability per unit of sales (as well as in aggregate) was proportional to market share or being a brand leader. This is still motivating many large companies today. General Electric, for example, sells off brands which are not first or second in their respective markets.

Such a strategy is not wrong (focus, after all, brings its own rewards) and there is certainly some relationship between market power and profitability. But at the time the finding was publicized, the link between market share and profitability was generally regarded as causal. Interestingly, Brad Gale, chief executive of PIMS at the time, has since concluded that these correlations were misleading – both market share and profitability are driven by the consumers' perceptions of quality.[6] But by then this new paradigm had already taken root. Thus marketing was seen as strategy – a zero sum game played by competitors. The logic underpinning it became, "my firm's market share will increase by the amount your firm loses."

The 1990s have brought recognition that competitive advantages are, generally, not sustainable, at least not by any effort of management. Environmental advantages, such as being one of the only two sources of diamonds, may be sustainable, but few firms are so well placed. As we discussed in Chapter 3, a constant cycle of innovation is needed. Arie de Geus, amongst others, has suggested that the *speed* of corporate (meaning managerial) learning is the only sustainable competitive advantage.[7]

In all this, the *relative* importance of the three Cs (Consumer, Competitor, and Company) passed largely unremarked. Having paid lip service to the consumer being king, the neoclassicist runs regressions on alternative (spending) options for the *company*. The conflict paradigm was obsessed with the *competitor*. Each rather missed the consumer perspective.

The vodka brand, Absolut, grew to the pre-eminent place in the US in the 1980s by building a special relationship with its consumers. It did this largely through advertising. The price was far beyond Smirnoff's, the brand leader. As it turned out, Brad Gale was right: share and profit were both driven by the consumers' perceptions of brand quality. The actual quality difference between the two brands, if any, is open to debate. It was enough that the consumer perceived Absolut to be better than Smirnoff. The marketers of Absolut were indifferent to Smirnoff's activities.

Smirnoff's marketers, meanwhile, were transfixed by all other vodkas. They wanted to dominate the *category*. When they were not worrying about their cheaper competitors, and doing deals to reduce the gap, they were worrying about the more expensive brands and trying to offer "value." Absolut felt free to raise prices throughout the 80s; Smirnoff barely moved at all. Smirnoff piled inventory into the trade to meet short-term sales and share targets.

Absolut soared and Smirnoff stagnated.

In the 1990s, excessive concern with competition gave way to the recognition that marketing is ultimately a matter of brand–consumer relationships, where the word "brand" is widely defined to include, for example, the firm marketing itself or the individual commodity. Relationship marketing, as it became known, emerged from industrial and services marketing and distribution channels where buyer–seller connections were personal and one-on-one. This was extended to direct marketing where databases could be used to give communications a personalised characteristic. The relational paradigm sees marketing not as a zero sum but as a win-win game where both consumers and competitive marketers benefit. This is why it is essentially co-operative rather than competitive.

Relationship marketing is far from new. Here is Karl Marx in 1867: "The difficulty with a *commodity* is that, like all categories of the capitalist mode of production, it represents a personal relationship under a material wrapping."[8] He continues with an exposé of exchange theory not far from marketing analysis over a century later.

Or consider China where *guanxi* (connections) is a relatively new (twentieth century) word but the concept captures generations of Chinese business practice. Westerners can find doing business with the Chinese frustrating because of their commitment to doing business only with established members of their own network. Deng Xiaoping's market reforms set in place a branded revolution but relationships remain the denominating factor.

In summary, we have three marketing approaches: competition (War), relationships (Empathy) and neoclassical (Math). That is not the order in which they arose, except in China, but, as we will see, the sequence in which they should be applied. If Roger Adams had embraced this more comprehensive approach, he would have first built shared experiences with his German counterparts before trying to sell them "research" in which they had no interest.

Now let us take another step into the human mind.

## Beliefs

Leon Festinger, a social psychologist, examined the relationship between facts, beliefs, and decision making in his doctoral thesis in the 1950s. He and his colleagues at the University of Minneapolis analyzed religious sects who prophesized cataclysmic events, e.g. on a given date, California would, so to speak, fall off the continent and be flooded. One group was preparing for such a "doomsday" when they would be rescued by flying saucers. Athough their expectations (predictions) failed to materialise, their false (to outsiders) beliefs not only prevailed but were magnified and the sect was strengthened. This was very odd. Those who left the sect were replaced by new believers in the prophecy, which had been post-rationalised into new dates.

Beliefs are strengthened both by the social group and by behavior. In the case of the sects studied, the reinforcement was not the experience of the event (which never took place) but the behavior, the actions and preparations in *anticipation* of the event. The actions of the believers help to shape their belief about the future. For example, the decision to sell their houses and quit their jobs was driven by their belief in the cataclysm to come, and those acts also *reinforced* those beliefs. Reason was used to support these convictions – in the same way we all justify our beliefs.

In marketing, successful first overseas ventures work in exactly this way. The decision owes more to commitment (beliefs) and the first-hand gathering of experience (memories) and relationships than to the rational processing of objective information. Commitment (belief) is reinforced by behavior and the selective perceptions of the exporter. It may be naive but it works.

Studies of these sects led Festinger, in the late 1950s, to the theory of cognitive dissonance. In brief, the theory consists of the notion that the human organism tries to establish internal harmony, consistency or congruity among his opinions, attitudes, knowledge, and values. To accommodate his theory, Festinger suggested that "cognition be decomposable into elements or, at least, clusters of elements." These "elements," sometimes irrelevant to one another, at other times follow from one another.

From his observations, Festinger concluded that, "If two [cognitive] elements are dissonant [out of harmony] with one another, the magnitude of the dissonance will be a function of the importance of the elements." And also that, "the total amount of dissonance between this element and the remainder of the person's cognition will depend on the proportion of relevant elements that are dissonant with the one in question."

In other words, if beliefs are strongly held both as important, and as "supported" by a wide range of social and behavioral inputs, they will override otherwise convincing facts.[9]

## How rational is decision making?

Western managers are brought up to believe that decision making is, or should be, rational. Economists claim that consumers, too, are ultimately rational whatever short-term appearances may indicate. The basic model of reasoning has been I(nformation) → C(ognitive processes) → B(ehavior). The cognitive (thinking) processes follow a series of logical steps (e.g. problem recognition, situation assessment, short-listing of alternatives, establishment of choice criteria, evaluation and selection). This sequence is now called into question.

In the West (the East was spared), "The Age of Enlightenment" was founded on the belief that, as W.S. Gilbert put it, "cool and calm consideration disentangles every plot." Reason saved mankind from its "animal spirits," which Descartes saw as particles in our (hot) blood that we shared with lower mammals. Our brains, graced with cool reason, were the essence of our existence and distinguished us from animals. Descartes' biology and etymology were both wrong. "Animal spirits," a medieval term, was derived from "anima" (the soul or living essence), not four-legged furry things.

To the Cartesian supremacy of reason over emotions, the seventeenth century added Newtonian mechanics, which became an organizing principle of educated thought. The very equations of economics were built explicitly on these mathematical foundations. Logic was king.

In the 1930s, Keynes saw that economics did not, in fact, explain wealth generation. On the contrary, wealth came from entrepreneurs doing things that had no economic justification. A great reader of Descartes, he turned animal spirits from vanquished to victor. Specifically, he saw them as the "spontaneous urge to action rather than inaction, and not as the outcome of a weighted average of quantitative benefits multiplied by quantitative probabilities."[10] Animal spirits were the source of wealth, *despite* reasoned analysis. Animal spirits are manifested in various ways: energy, vitality, power and the determination to act. Animal spirits, then, are closely associated with decision making and implementation. The Chinese distinguish two varieties, though the same two characters are used for both. Jingshén refers to the spirit, akin to anima. Without the rising tone it means vigour, vitality and drive.

The digital revolution and computer technology both complicate and simplify the picture. During World War II, Cambridge mathematician, Alan Turing, set out to model our brains' logical processes in order to understand German war codes ("enigma"). For Turing, speed was critical. More recently, artificial intelligence experts have been trying to mimic the human brain through computer technology: pattern recognition, neural networks, and adaptive/learning systems, for example. We now know that computers as models of the mind is erroneous for we are only reading what we ourselves have projected into memory. In recent times we find computer toys and robots "expressing" spontaneous initiative, a phenomenon called "emergent behavior." However spontaneous and unpredictable this behavior appears, it is still programmed and is not beyond human control. Through neurobiology and related sciences we know that human and computer memories work in very different ways. If we review a human memory, for example, the memory is changed as a result. A computer that stores memory, however, always stays the same unless it is destroyed or reprocessed.

If the technicians really could build a machine to mimic the brain's functions, they would abandon their present unique focus on logic connections. Computers are beginning to excel at copying the way we think and analyze but are hopeless at feelings, relationships and creativity. They complicate our business through senseless rationality, like sending bills for $0.00, but they simplify our futures as we can leave thinking and remembering to them while we have fun with feelings and networking.

The dominance of cognition has been implicitly and explicitly challenged from various academic research schools. Both cognitive psychology and medical neuroscience find that the links between individual feelings, social behavior, and decision making do not necessarily involving thinking. It is such research that serves to reunite body with mind animal instincts with logical processes in decision making; in other words, a strong argument for the irrational.

As we know, business schools have found challenges to rationality uncomfortable: an authoritative book, *The Irrational Executive*, which reviews how business decisions were *really* made, was not borrowed from the Columbia Business School library in the first 12 years that it sat there.

## The MAC model

In the world of international marketing, doubts about the ICB (rational sequence of Information, Cognition, Behaviour) model of decision making arise from many sources:

- *The personal precedes the analytical.* Our experience, along with that of many executives, indicates that, time and again, managers build decisions on their own personal experience and affective personal relationships before taking objective information on board, if indeed they do so at all.

- *Fancy often prevails over facts.* As Festinger showed, some decisions owe more to beliefs than to objective information. To reduce dissonance, information was used selectively to support beliefs. Rosemary Kalapurakal found the same phenomenon when researching the use of competitive price information by supermarket buyers. The research was impeccable and yet the buyers rejected it when it failed to match their beliefs. London Business School Professor Patrick Barwise, and colleagues found that strategic investment decisions were made quickly and then extensive analysis took place to formalize matters.[11]

- *Animal spirits prevail over economic theory.* Relationship marketing implies that the relationship itself is more than a net present value of economic outcomes. That such an eminent economist as Keynes recognised animal spirits as the driver of decisions, is significant. Some modern economists have begun to follow that trail, though whether they are employing the right maps is open to challenge.

- *Sensing prevails over thinking.* The evidence from the sciences increasingly points to a more sophisticated model of decision making than provided by just logical (neocortical) processing. The most important is Antonio Damasio's research, which concluded that decision making in the brain is co-located with feelings, not thinking.[12] Damasio is a neuro-scientist who derived this finding from brain-damaged patients past and present. Of course, damaged locations do not prove the case for undamaged people. But independent work, using brain scans on healthy subjects, notably that by Professor Larry Cahill and colleagues at Irvine, California, supports Damasio's conclusion.

The evidence points overwhelmingly to decision making being, at most, partially cognitive. More of it is driven by memory (experience, habit, virtual reality helmets) and one's feelings (affect). The co-location of these senses and social skills or consideration may be significant. It seems likely that decisions are driven by not only how we feel but also by our social network, but we do not know for sure.

Since this runs counter to so much of our upbringing, we should stop to ask whether it *should* be thus. Perhaps, as Descartes saw it, our animal spirits just have more hold over us than we anticipated. We just have to rise further to pure reason. This is to suggest that computers are better decision makers. For some things they are. If the dealer is not shuffling the deck, computers will track the changing odds on two pairs or a full house better than humans, and bet accordingly. But they cannot intuit. They cannot use implicit and social information. Their decision making is limited to set programming, so the concept that rational decision making is primary, is misguided. In reaching decisions and making choices, rational considerations are, at most, just a part of the process.

The MAC model of marketing decision making is derived from a number of research disciplines sign-posted above, especially Damasio's work in neurobiology, and in advertising. How advertising works is beyond the scope of this chapter but it does highlight the primacy of experience and habit (technically, memory) over rational thought.

Specifically, the MAC model assumes that humans, be they managers or consumers, make most decisions on the basis of memory. Think of your last visit down a supermarket aisle. Choices were barely conscious. They were, mostly, quick and automatic. Recall how annoyed we get when the layout changes and we have to think.

Some choices need more than memory. We have three levels of emotion from weak to strong. Mood is background; feelings are mild sensations of pleasure or disagreeableness. Primal emotions are dominant, somatic, adrenalin-rousing sensations of hate, love, or fear. These occupy different parts of the human brain. "Affect" is used here to refer to the middle level, feelings, and is co-located with social skills on the underside of the front lobes.

If memory will not suffice, we do what feels right. Those who have lost this part of their brain are unable to make decisions. Finally, if memory and affect together do not suffice, for example the partners in a business relationship feel differently, cognition (rational thought) comes into play.

As Festinger suggested, cognition is quite often used to resolve dissonance *after* the decision is made. We rationalise the condominium we have just bought, when our decision was based mainly on considerations of personal taste and comfort. Affect first, logic second.

This, admittedly, understates the importance of cognition in the business context. Most firms do calculate the cost and benefits of key decisions at some stage. If the chosen option does not look good, it is untangled.

This should not surprise any executive who has encountered analysis paralysis. For some managers, there is always a need to seek more information, more data, before a decision should – note the "should" – be made. Cartesians are wrong in seeing reason as a badge of superiority.

Affect (feelings) must operate within the context of experience, memories and habits. If we took Damasio at face value, our model would simply be M providing the context for A. This would not be realistic: we all employ analysis whenever the decision is difficult. The analysis may not dictate the choice but, at the minimum, it can be helpful whether it is to resolve the decision or to reduce subsequent cognitive dissonance. Where the decision is a group choice, we employ logical arguments to debate the alternatives.

The MAC model is, like any model, a highly simplified version of reality. We all differ and choose differently at different times. In our brains, M, A, and C are highly interactive.

Cartesians might counter that decision making may be based on feelings, but they would be better if they were rational. This is the argument we touched on earlier, that rationality is normative, the way things *should* be. Leaving aside arguments that the world should be square, the debate turns on which works better in practice. Do decisions based entirely on rational, quantitative considerations make firms more successful than MAC-type approaches? By "successful" we mean that firms have achieved their own objectives *and* impressed outsiders by superior performance.

*We all differ and choose differently at different times*

Definitive research is in its infancy but early indications, as we will see later, support the MAC model, at least for international marketing. So did, in effect, Keynes.

There are good, relational reasons why this should be. Business is not a game of chess where each player sits alone calculating the optimal moves. International marketing, in particular, develops from human co-operation. It is social, as the Chinese recognized, before it is economic. Risk may be a matter of computation, but more often it is measured in terms of comfort. As relationships strengthen, trust and commitment increase and greater risk becomes tolerable. Thus, in the relational perspective, M(emory) is building up and provides context for A(ffect). Rational decisions (C) will need to be made but, again, only within the MA framework.

*Business is not a game of chess where each player sits alone calculating the optimal moves*

As those fresh out of business school discover, trying to use a strictly cognitive model in a MAC environment causes misunderstanding and frustration. In other words, if MAC is normal, it is also normative.

The MAC model explains decision making in the global market. Specifically, while market entry decisions are often influenced by rational considerations, they take place only in the context of experience and how individual managers feel about the options and how they develop their business networks. More generally, the MAC model underpins the relational paradigm of marketing. Our social skills and networks, and our mental processes, determine not only how marketing processes and decisions do take place but also how they should.

## The MAC model and market research

In the Cartesian view, market research is essential, perhaps the *sine qua non*, in providing the raw material for decisions. The consumer's decision making in this view follows the ICB chain of reasoning; so if the marketer can understand what I(nformation) produces what B(ehavior), he can adjust the I in order to obtain the desired B. The mental processing is rational and bounded only by the information available and the consumer's ability (e.g. time constraints and competitive information) to process it.

Let us consider how this reasoning may lead us astray.

Suppose the manager can produce thermometers for refrigerators in either pink or blue. There are no financial considerations and, to a rationalist, the choice for the consumer is trivial. Anyway, he researches and finds a 60/40 preference for blue. Blue thermometers are duly launched. Sales then under-perform because:

- Fashion changes during the months between research and launch.
- Consumers cannot predict their future behavior.
- Competition did the same research and launched blue as well.

Bad example? It happens all the time.

Future pricing and product features research tell similar stories. For example, Dave Krysiek's experience of traditional (cognitive) measures in the car and credit card businesses indicated that they did not differentiate between users.[13] Later research with projective techniques for General Motors, Saab, and Visa distinguished the groups on attitudinal and social attributes (A). For example, in the Saab research, Mercedes users were seen as "snobby show-offs" and Volvo as "boring, 2.3 kids and a dog." Interestingly, both users and non-users of the cars saw themselves in much the same way. Volvo drivers admitted to being boring. Thus the affective dimension of decision making correctly allocated customer types to cars, whereas the economic analysis failed.

In practice there are many reasons for commissioning research, some political, as a recent forum of US market research experts testified:

"*Mr Neal:* 'If we're successful, the marketing manager takes the credit. And if the product fails or the segmentation doesn't work, they blame the researcher. That's reality ...'

*Ms Hisiger:* 'Except that research is typically a forward-looking process. By the time a product comes to market, [original] management may be long gone.'"[14]

Research plays a large part in international marketing and we will look at political aspects later. The question here is why it is unreliable. That arises from a false understanding of consumer decision making and how consumers respond to rational questions and surveys.

Let us suppose you are the export manager of an Italian firm making white widgets. The white widget market in Italy is strong. The French also have a large widget market, but all their widgets are black. The Italian company sees an opportunity for its product in France and conducts research using question-and-answer surveys. French consumers reject the idea of white widgets; black ones are fine. The Italian production team says that black widgets would be too costly to be competitive. Do you accept that and keep out of France, or research grey widgets, or sell black ones to establish your brand in France, or ignore the research and market the white ones anyway?

The truth is that the French consumers have no experience of white widgets. They are giving cognitive responses to cognitive questions. Hypothetical research of this type is routinely unreliable.

To establish the size of the French white widget market, greater subtlety is required. You may find French consumers in Italy and ask them. You may test the market in France by selling a few to establish actual experience with white widgets. At least, you should run supervised product usage trials where the respondents may try the widgets and discuss them with their peers under the direction of a psychologist. Remember that you are looking for the way they *feel* about the white widgets, not the logical, and probably disparaging, things they now *say*.

One of the most encouraging aspects about Bailey's Irish Cream, now the world's leading liqueur, was that it failed all its market research tests. Consumers had never encountered anything like it and, accordingly, rejected it. The moral of the widget story is not to accept any research until it is based on experience (M and A).

Jeffrey Hartley, a key member of General Motors' research team in Warren, MI, distinguishes "customer-inspired" from "customer-defined" products with a chilling tale of the results of creating an oil painting through market research.[15] Customers defined, through survey responses, what they liked best in a picture to hang in their living room. A painting was then created, based on these preferences, and was disliked by everyone.

General Motors sets out to align customer and company minds. The company is made up of many people and even the most tightly targeted customer segment is still diverse. Their first stage is a range of in depth methods, e.g. focus groups, observations of product usage and debriefing new users, to get to "know" the customer. Their toolbox includes about 20 less traditional methods. They have to balance listening too closely (and producing lousy oil paintings) with reducing risk and uncertainty.

This example highlights the need for developing customer *empathy*. Market research is never foolproof, but asking about consumer *experience* (what they actually did) is more reliable than their *feelings* (or attitudes), which are hard to communicate without being disrupted by cognition, especially in Descartes' home country. US academic, Tim Wilson, and colleagues conducted research that shows why attitude behavior correlation (ABC) has always been so bad (80 percent wrong is a rule of thumb) in advertising research.[16] Consumers don't do what their reported attitudes indicate they should do. Quite often, attitudes are altered by the mere act of questioning those attitudes.

Thus researching consumers is helped by recognising the MAC model with its focus on experience and feelings. Keep away from inviting the consumer to rationalise, and from hypothetical questions about future behavior. Rather, give them experiential opportunities (M) and empathize with how they feel (A).

# Executive notes

In this chapter we have examined how marketing, as well as consumer buying decisions, are made; both marketers supplying and consumers buying. We have not differentiated between the two.

In particular we have reviewed:

- Ethnocentricity. Global media have made it easier to become immersed in Western attitudes and forget the realities of other cultures. National success reinforces a national mindset which builds barriers against international understanding. Thus within success lie the seeds of failure

- Virtual reality helmets. We make choices using processes ingrained by culture and upbringing. Professional training encourages us to believe our minds work in the "right" way in all settings

- The three ways of thinking about marketing are the neoclassical (Math), strategy (War) and relational (Empathy). This is the order in which they emerged historically but the third harks back to the fundamental principle of marketing which is to serve end users and profit by meeting their needs before one's own. Accordingly, it is the most important

- Beliefs. Many decisions are belief driven with objective information used to reduce cognitive dissonance and justify prior choices

- Rationality. At some risk of over-simplification, we reduced the rational decision model to ICB: I(nformation) → C(ognition) → B(ehavior);

- The MAC (Memory → Affect → Cognition) model includes a feedback loop for experience. Cognition (thinking) plays a part, but within the context of feelings, which are more significant for decision making. Both are dominated by experience (memory)

- Market research. Finally, we took a brief look at why some market research is unreliable for market entry

Marketing decisions take all shapes and sizes. We do not intend to leave the impression that they can all be reduced to one simple model, nor that rationality, analysis or logic do not matter. The international marketer needs all the tools there are. Our purpose was different: over time we have subscribed unknowingly to barriers that keep out the ways other people choose. Such barriers are dangerous. We use MAC principles in later chapters.

# References

1. Debray, R. (1980) *Revolution in the Revolution?* Westport Connecticut: Greenwood Press, p. 19.
2. Shakespeare, W. *Julius Caesar*. Mark Antony to the crowd, Act III, Scene ii.
3. Melcher, R. *et al.* (1992) "The New Managers for the New Europe," *Business Week*, 14 September, p. 45.
4. Kotler, P. (1990) "From Transactions to Relationships to Networks," Address to the Trustees of the Marketing Science Institute (November), *MSI Review*, Spring 1991.
5. Kotler, P. (1997) *Marketing Management: Analysis, planning and control*. 9th edn. Upper Saddle River, NJ: Prentice Hall, p. 12.
6. Gale, B. (1994) "The Importance of Market-Perceived Quality," in Stobart, P. (ed) *Brand Power*. London and Basingstoke: Macmillan.
7. de Geus, A. P. (1988) "Planning as Learning," *Harvard Business Review*, March–April.
8. Marx, K. (1867) "The Process of Capitalist Production," *Capital*, Vol.1 Book 1. Moscow: Foreign Languages Publishing House, 1954, p. 84.
9. Festinger, L. (1957) *A Theory of Cognitive Dissonance*. Stanford, CA: Stanford University Press.
10. Keynes, J. M. (1936) *The General Theory of Employment, Interest and Money*. London: Macmillan, p. 161.
    Matthews, R. (1991) "Animal Spirits," in Tulip Meeks, J. G. (ed) *Thoughtful Economic Man*. Cambridge: Cambridge University Press, 103–25.
11. Barwise, P. *et al.* (1986) "Research on Strategic Investment Decisions" in McGee J. and Thomas H. (eds) *Strategic Management Research: A European perspective*, 17: 99–120.
12. Damasio, A. R. (1994) *Descartes' Error*. London: Papermac, Macmillan.
13. "Measurable Marketing," presentation to an Institute for International Research Seminar. Atlanta, 19 February, 1999.
14. *Marketing News*. Chicago: American Marketing Association, 5 Jan, 1998, p. 9.
15. Hartley, J. (1996) "Aligning the Customer and the Company Minds," presentation at Marketing Science Conference, Florida, February.
16. Wilson, T. *et al.* (1989) "Introspection, Attitude Change, and Attitude-Behavior Consistency: The Disruptive Effects of Explaining Why We Feel the Way We Do," in Berkowitz, L. (ed) *Advances in Experimental Social Psychology*, Vol. 22. New York: Academic Press, 287–343.

# Organizational learning

## International planning processes

'You can do what you want
If you don't think you can't
So don't think you can't think you can'
*Source:* Inge on Coué[1]


'Lieutenant-General Grant,
Not expecting to see you again before the spring campaign opens,
I wish to express in this way my entire satisfaction with what you
have done up to this time, so far as I understand it. The particulars
of your plans I neither know nor seek to know. You are vigilant and
self-reliant; and, pleased with this, I wish not to obtrude any
constraints or restraints upon them. While I am very anxious that
any great disaster or capture of our men in great numbers shall be
avoided, I know these points are less likely to escape your attention
than they would mine. If there is anything wanting which is within
my power to give, do not fail to let me know it. And now, with a
brave army and a just cause, may God sustain you.
Yours very truly,
A. Lincoln'[2]

We portray the international marketer as a manager who works between national units, juggling the roles of butterfly and bee, one who plays within the "white" spaces of creativity, between image and knowledge. Let us now give our marketer another balancing act. Perhaps nowhere must he play with greater agility than upon the fields of strategy.

For our purposes, strategy retains its Greek meaning: it is what military generals do. This covers three separate activities: designing a battle plan, ensuring that the troops and munitions are adequately supplied, and providing leadership.

After some distinctions to better define the field of battle, we begin with reconnaissance and positioning. We will not enquire further into resourcing: that should be covered by the plan. We return to leadership when we encounter PASSION: creating passion is the leader's primary role. This chapter, therefore, concerns planning.

Planning is useful insofar as:

- It changes the *minds* of the team that will carry out the plan: stretching for the impossible, stimulating motivation, commitment, and team-work.
- It changes what the firm actually *does,* i.e. resource allocation and making choices.

When does planning begin? It depends on the business. If you plan to build refineries for the next 10 years, you will need 10-year plans. By and large, however, most multinationals begin far too early and continue long after planning makes no difference. Worthwhile planning needs to precede execution by only one step. Marketers would manage better with a single one-year combined plan and budget. Curiously, planning can become addictive. When GrandMet (now Diageo) tried in 1996/7 to reduce forecasting and planning, its divisions carried on regardless. Both planning, and complaining about it, had become institutionalized.

Most international firms could improve their plans and save entire forests by integrating their planning processes with training, new projects, working parties, and initiatives. All of these activities are ways of rehearsing the future. Firms regard them as wholly separate but they should be combined. As a result, they have initiative overload, training budget deficits, and scrambled plans.

# Planning at General Electric

General Electric (GE), in the 1970s, developed the classic planning system to a high order. The company had very high knowledge of its businesses but perhaps too low a perception of environmental change. In market after market, GE was beaten to the draw. As a result, the central planning system, with its piles of paper and separate existence, was scrapped. Coincidentally, GE's emphasis switched to training and development.

To reinforce communication for cultural change, all managers were to attend the company's Management Development Institute in Crotonville, New York. At these sessions, Welch explained his vision and engaged in a no-holds-barred give-and-take question and debate session about GE. The success of these sessions encouraged Welch to replicate this interaction in a process in which all employees could participate. This initiative was termed Work-Out.

The concept was a forum where a cross-section of employees could speak their minds about the management of their business without the fear of retribution by their superiors. Employees could get immediate action on their recommendations. Welch viewed it as a tool of change, particularly in challenging the bureaucracy and redefining management's roles and relationships:

"Work-Out has a practical and intellectual goal. The practical objective is to get rid of thousands of bad habits accumulated since the creation of GE. The second thing we want to achieve, the intellectual part, begins by putting the leaders in front of 100 or so of their people, eight to ten times a year, to let them know what their people think. Work-Out sessions will expose the leaders to the vibrations of their business – opinions, feelings, emotions, and resentments, not abstract theories of organisation and management."

Over a period of one year, eight to ten studies were carried out by GE managers as part of their training. A range of new ideas from these companies was identified. Examples include asset management from Digital, product development from Honda, quality improvement from Hewlett Packard and customer service from American Express.

*Sources:* "GE Chief Hopes to Shape Agile Giant," *L.A. Times*, 1 June 1988
Stewart, T. A., "GE Keeps Those Ideas Coming," *Fortune*, 12 August 1991.
Tichy, N. and Charan, R. "Speed Simplicity and Self Confidence. An interview with Jack Welch," *Harvard Business Review*, Sept/Oct. 1989

Planning should be a team game where many futures are considered and the best chosen. The process should be enjoyable, the planners working more under A. Lincoln's than M. Coué's exhortations, quoted at the start of the chapter, but both capture a key objective of the planning process: motivation. If done well, planning contributes to higher performance; absorbing new information reveals how to achieve the impossible and the motivation enhances the appetite for it.

*Planning should be a team game where many futures are considered and the best chosen*

Plans do not have to be written down – either on paper or in cyberspace – but they do need to be explicit. Value comes from rendering the implicit explicit and we cannot internationalize, i.e. learn across borders, without this clarity. Stage C of the SILK cycle (dissemination) has to be explicit information. A plan represents the minutes of a meeting of minds. Like any other minutes, all the options discussed do not need description: just who will do what, when and at what cost and benefit, and with what assumptions.

Research tells us that, in general, planning is positively associated with performance.[3] In export marketing, for example, planning has been identified as a discriminator between successful exporters and non-exporters.[4] We suggest that to assess the level of resources needed, and to get the best from them, managers need to:

- Integrate planning, training, and initiatives into a single, simplified annual cycle.
- Plan together in teams, not separately by function, division or technical specialty.
- For the main annual plan, imagine as many futures as each unit needs until it finds one that is acceptable.
- Share those goals internationally in order to learn and improve across borders.
- Then stop.

Although this book is concerned primarily with inter-market linkage, we need to revisit how single market units should plan using the War, Empathy, Math sequence. Then we can see how these plans can provide learning for the whole group.

The single market planning process should sequentially involve all three perspectives of marketing (*see* Chapter 4): War (strategy), Empathy (relational) and Math (microeconomic). One perspective does not superimpose upon, nor replace, another.

The sequence matters. As shown in Figure 5.1, *War* provides the rough-cutting of strategy. It is drastic but quick. *Empathy*, the incremental building of relationships, is by contrast slow and demands patience. Killing those to whom you have spent years sending red roses is clearly a waste of resources. Make war first and love second.

That said, the implicit to explicit path of value extraction does not ignore the need for control. Plans need to be quantified financially before they are accepted and implemented. A plan that *feels* wonderful may prove disastrous once the numbers are added up. *Math* has its place. Modern sophisticates regard the traditional 4Ps approach as inward looking, uncreative, old fashioned, and rationalist. So it is. So is arithmetic. But if you expect to see any change from your $100 bill, learn to do the necessary sums.

Thus, the complete process is War → Empathy → Math (WEM).

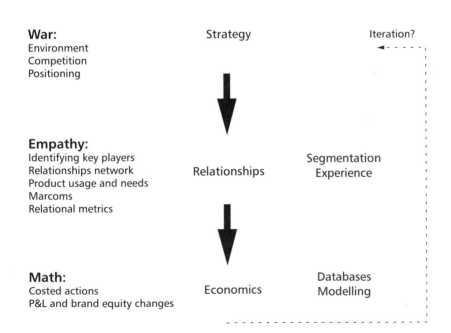

**Fig. 5.1    The WEM planning sequence**

Notice how this corporate decision-making process is similar to MAC for individuals, so far as the second and third stages are concerned. Empathy (Affect) and rational math (Cognition), have much in common.

Measurement forms Chapter 7, so let us focus now on War and Empathy.

## War

'In our ten years of war two deviations often arose ...
one was to belittle the enemy, the other was to be terrified of him'

*Source:* Mao Tse-Tung[5]

## Drive international market development for innovative consumer products

Thomas's Europe is a fast-growing part of the global Mars organisation and an established market leader in its own right. We make a wide variety of products for international petcare markets, many of them under the world-famous Pedigree and Whiskas brand names. These include an innovative and fast-developing range of food, health and accessory products, whose sales are currently growing around 17 per cent a year. As part of a team responsible for mainland Europe your challenge will be to increase their market penetration.

Spending up to three-quarters of your time outside the UK, you'll need to gain a full understanding of the various markets, channels and competition before developing strategies and practical proposals for the launch or extension of carefully-targeted product portfolios. In mature markets you'll work closely with colleagues in local Mars businesses to devise and implement effective programmes, while in emerging markets you'll handle everything from initial research to planning, setting up and monitoring local distribution operations.

*Source:* job advertisement in *The Sunday Times*, 17 January 1998

War is expensive. Wise commanders protect their resources in various ways:

- Knowing the terrain, the sizes and locations of the enemy and who and where friends are
- Knowing which enemies and customers really matter. Where there are too many to consider individually, can they be grouped into segments or taken as a whole?
- In the light of that, taking the most advantageous ground, i.e. positioning. Being *different* has two advantages: it provides a reason for customers to like you and a reason for competitors not to dislike you. From their point of view, the more different your brand, the better for their brands. They might even ignore you completely. Ignorance is bliss; fighting may be fatal
- Distinguishing two types of engagement: tactical battles or skirmishes, and total war. The skirmish, as guerrilla leaders well know, is designed to increase your weaponry (resources) at the expense of your enemy's. You are not really fighting, just improving the balance of resources. In a skirmish you can be weak: it will be hit and run. Virgin, for example, made an issue of the proposed BA and American Airlines merger: they were not committing to fight so much as taking advantage of the media opportunity. Total war is the opposite: only start when you are sure to win. Be bigger than the enemy and ensure he stays dead
- Focus. War is won by concentrating the most firepower on confined space at exactly the right time. The size of space available for attack is dictated by the firepower relative to the competition

Marketers break these simple rules all the time. Reconnaissance is inadequate, positioning is fuzzy and diffuse, smaller brands frontally attack bigger brands and start price wars they cannot win, and promotional material arrives too late. Most plans attempt too much with too little. Take another look at your own.

*Most plans attempt too much with too little*

In this section, we simply address two key stages: reconnaissance and, in the light of that, positioning.

As the international marketer, you are entitled to expect that national units have done their own reconnaissance and are familiar with their Environments, Customers, Competitors and their own Company's competencies

(E+3Cs). The international manager will review these analyses, probably orally, mostly to learn, but also to be sure they are thoroughly done.

## Environment

Analysis of the macro-environment, i.e. socio-economic factors, frames the firm's options. The environment may be defined as all those things the marketer should be aware of but can *do* nothing about. Factor them into plans, do not worry about them. Anxiety should be reserved for the things one can change. This, in essence, is the Tao: fixing what can be fixed and then accepting one's fate in a relaxed way.

Finding the right "match" between the environment and the firm has long been a concern of the strategist. The well-known SWOT analysis – Strengths, Weaknesses (of the firm), Opportunities, Threats (posed by the environment) – was developed at Harvard Business School and epitomises this approach. SWOT analysis should be more interesting than it usually proves to be. Our experience is that it quickly descends to generalities and reinforces introversion. Nevertheless SWOT, like Porter's Five Forces model, remains enduringly popular and, if it works for you, it works.

Matching strategy to environment becomes more difficult as the pace of environmental change increases. By the time we think we have a strategy, conditions have changed. 3M requires its managers to spend time working *outside* strategy because by the time strategy is recognized as such, it is already middle-aged. Long lead times in product development and test marketing compound the problem. Firms increasingly opt for speed over precision. Realistically and creatively looking into the future, using scenario techniques, for example, can be helpful, fun, and provide a context for imagination and learning.

## Customer

Quite often, customers cannot articulate what they need or want in clear language. The standard textbook advice that end user's needs and problems are the right place to start is difficult, if not impossible, in practice. Major brand successes, such as the familiar Post-it Notes, flow from a creative connection between product and consumers that is not immediately obvious, i.e. outsights.

In an article in *The Times*, Sir George Bull, then chairman of Grand Met and a long-time marketer, decried the fact that, "many marketers now shelter behind their pile of numbers" – trying to replace the art of marketing with the science of number crunching.[6] Bull cites Bailey's Irish Cream, one of Ireland's biggest exports, as an example of how a successful marketing idea was born over lunch. No research. No competitive analysis.

Those of an analytic disposition invest much time and effort in "understanding the consumer" through mountains of research reports. The MAC model, by contrast, suggests empathizing with the consumer by shelving the paperwork and getting out to share customer experience. Do what consumers do, mix with them, and see what they see. Then, and only then, read a few reports to structure your thinking.

## Competitor

From an analysis of customer needs and wants, planning turns its attention to the competition. How well are those needs being met now and prospectively by competitors? Unsatisfied needs can provide valuable insights but they rarely arise from competitors' product comparisons. Lilac carrots may not exist now but that does not imply there is a market for them. At any point in time, the market is fully supplied and shelves are loaded. Spaces represent only temporary out-of-stocks. The regular suppliers will have them back in stock before your truck leaves your gate. Discovering new space owes more to imagination than product analysis and more to differentiation than imitation. Market gaps are created by great new products just as a ship makes space for itself by forging through the waves. The wake is only apparent with hindsight.

Competitive analysis helps show what should *not* be done, for example what competitors are doing wrong so you can avoid the same mistakes. But it rarely tells you what you should be doing instead. As the late Sir James Goldsmith pointed out, by the time you see a bandwagon, you have missed it. Conversely, if you are large enough, watch what pioneers do, and then do it bigger and better. There are plenty of examples of this paradox. Where they agree is to reject doing too little, too late.

## Company

The final element in the E+3Cs approach is the company's own capabilities. Important changes in the way this is understood have taken place in recent years. The focus on matching the firm with the competitive environment has been replaced partly by the "resource-based" view of the firm which focuses on the key internal elements of competitive advantage.[7] This approach has been popularised under the banner of "core competencies." Other labels include resources, invisible assets, strategic assets, distinctive capabilities and meta-skills.

According to Hamel and Prahalad, core competence has three characteristics:[8]

- Source of competitive advantage – makes them different
- Potential breadth of applications – across product forms
- Difficulty of competitor imitation – due to proprietary or tacit knowledge, for example.

Analysis of existing core competence, or distinctive capability, can be challenged as being circular reasoning (as noted in Chapter 3, commentators usually identify core competence from its *consequences* after they have happened). Comparing the consumer-valued competencies likely to be needed in tomorrow's world the company's current stock of resources and skills should force the firm to be brutally honest about what, if anything, it has or does that rivals do not have

*Development comes from what firms do not what they wish they were*

or cannot do. But, as in SWOT analysis, stop when it becomes another rain-dance.

## The positioning statement

Does the E+3Cs analysis help determine the best strategy? Like any other reconnaissance, it does not tell you what to do, only what to avoid. Positioning, however, is where the strategy rubber hits the marketing road. Any national or international marketing plan without this cornerstone should be rejected out of hand.

Gatorade™ produces sports drinks for physical activity enthusiasts who consider themselves to be accomplished, but not necessarily competitive, athletes. This offering provides benefits that satisfy our consumers' need to quench thirst in a healthy and fun (but not frivolous) way. Our offering uniquely attracts our target consumers because it is absorbed in the body 12 times faster than water and because it is heavily promoted using imagery of everyday athletes working up a sweat. Our benefits differ from competitors' benefits in the following ways: fun, scientifically-backed, quenching.

*Source:* Gatorade positioning statement

Al Ries and Jack Trout popularised "positioning" in the 1980s as *the few words that distinguish the brand from any other.*[9] Fifty years earlier, Rosser Reeves created a similar concept, the USP (unique selling proposition), now called the "differentiating advantage."[10] Pampers, for example, has been positioned as the "driest diaper." Procter & Gamble use "white box tests" to measure actual product (originally washing detergent) scores against competition, without help from its brand name.

We call this the "consumer proposition." Different firms use "positioning" with roughly similar meaning but varying formats. A full positioning statement needs more definition than merely a catch phrase.

*Positioning is where the strategy rubber hits the marketing road*

The brand should position itself in the most favorable slot in the consumer's mind. If another brand is already there, the marketer should position his offering somewhere else unless he can zap the incumbent (rare). Repositioning, remember, is difficult and expensive – it is the consumer, after all, who is doing the positioning in his own mind. It is one thing to lodge something into blank memory, quite another to move it.

The consumer proposition is not the advertising copy-line, e.g. "Life is a Sport, Drink it Up™," but the consumer's memory triggered by the communication stimulus, that is, where the consumer places your brand relative to the others available in the category. Gatorade would like it to be "the healthy, fun, thirst quencher." The ideal positioning is distinctive: a key question is, would one recognise the brand from an untitled proposition? For example, what famous US food brand is "… Easy, unpretentious fun and laughter. A magic transformation of something ordinary into something that exudes joy, delight and a special kind of fun!"?[11] If that was difficult, what US imported brand is: "A 4x4 vehicle with luxury"?[12]

The long-term dominance of brand leaders is due to the way memory is formed. Once synapses are created, they do not go away. Defending a brand positioning is more straightforward, and requires fewer resources, than attacking an existing position. New entrants more often find a *new position* (niche) and then seek to shift associations and attention to that. Occupying an empty hill takes fewer resources than attacking an occupied hill but can you get consumer attention to shift over there?

When all experiential, affective and cognitive factors have been taken into account, the positioning statement might well be too long: more than a single page *is* too long. This is not the time to please everyone. Effective positioning requires sacrifice. A brand that is all things to all people is nothing to anyone. The smaller and weaker a brand is, the narrower the focus, and the more the consequential sacrifice. Narrow focus is good practice for large brands too, but very large, extended brands such as Mitsubishi can sustain a broader proposition. Secondary targets and compromises should be abandoned in favour of maximizing firepower on the most tightly focused target. A positioning statement that is precise, clear, and likely to be successful can be written in less than a page – however big the brand.

In summary, a good positioning statement is:

- *Specific* – in the way it spells out the target group (can you picture this person?), benefit etc.
- *Easily communicated* – internally, to agencies and to target consumers (this avoids technical product managers over-complicating matters)
- *Consumer relevant* – speaks to a genuine consumer need and is believable
- *Highly valued* – the proposition is a big winner with the target consumer
- *Distinctive* – it stands out from everyone else in the category
- *Ownable* – could only be associated with your brand and is difficult to copy

- *Deliverable* – your firm has the capacity to live up to the brand's promise
- *Profitable* – the positioning must be mutually beneficial, i.e. the marketer has to get something out of this as well.

Table 5.1 summarizes the conventional headings. Sometimes key marketing mix strategies may be added if they are critical, e.g. distribution outlets for perfumes. We discuss later how the international manager reconciles different positionings for the same brand in different countries.

Once the brand positioning statement has been established in a few terse paragraphs, the brand's "essence" can be established. This captures in ten words or less (ideally two or three) the brand's individuality and life force. Smirnoff, in the early 1990s, for example, was reduced to "pure thrill." This is not a copy-line but the kernel of the brand from which communications can be developed.

Getting global buy-in to brand essence is a major undertaking requiring massive research. David Ogilvy started the idea by telling us to research a brand until it confesses its essence. The test, like positioning, is whether the phrase could apply to a competitor.

## Empathy

We now move from War to love, or Empathy. Remember that here we are concerned with relational planning in the international context. The process should build the strength and motivation of the trading relationships. Partners, such as distributors, will be quick to resist plans whose intent seems to be control.

When J&B Rare became successful in the United States, the importer, Abe Rosenberg, resented any form of planning or control. Rosenberg would order product as he sold it and pay when he was paid. What else would an exporter need to know? Even in the late 1960s, 30 years later, a sales forecast could be obtained only grudgingly on the back of an envelope. The fact that Scotch whisky took four years to mature, that US volume was two million cases with a 20 percent market share, were seen as the exporter's problems.

**Table 5.1    Brand positioning statement**

*Category*.   How the marketer defines the type of offering. Consumers need cues to retrieve the right "category map." Categories may be organized by product types, e.g. banking, soap powder, or by some other organizing scheme, e.g. all things that help me to get going in the morning, such as Folgers coffee and Zest soap.

*Partner consumer*.   A term preferred to the more conventional "target consumer" which denotes hostility.

*Consumer proposition*.   A very brief distinguishing phrase that summarises "what's in it for the consumer," i.e. key benefit. Benefits can be, of course, primarily functional (reliability – Volkswagen, stain removal – Tide), psychological (self-concept enhancing – Calvin Klein) or they can emphasize economic/value benefits (lowest airfares – ValueJet/EasyJet). This necessarily requires sacrifice.

*Support*.   How is your brand able to provide its benefit? Does the consumer proposition draw upon specific product features, the brand's heritage and imagery, or its price?

*Target competitor*.   Which is the brand from which you aim to take most business? Too many targets mean no target. What would the consumer buy if your brand was out of stock?

*Differentiation*.   Why, and how, is your brand different from the rest of the category/the target competitor? Do you offer a different benefit, or do you deliver the same benefit differently?

*Preference*.   Why is your brand better from the consumer's, or end user's, point of view? The "shopping aisle" test (or equivalent in your category) is a good way to sharpen this section of the positioning statement. Imagine the consumer picks the target competitor's product off the shelf and you have about five seconds to provide a compelling reason to switch to yours before she moves on to her next category purchase. Five seconds may not seem long, but a proposition that takes much longer is probably unclear, not well focused or too complex.

The moral of the J&B story is not the frustration experienced by whisky makers and accountants but the empathy and the strong relationship that existed between Rosenberg and the J&B team in London. They could see the market through his eyes and make their own forecasts.

In planning for a national market, the team needs to empathize with two types of customer: the immediate trade buyer for the "push" part of the strategy and the end user for the "pull." In chain retailing, Burger King for example, store managers and franchisees take the place of trade buyers.

To simplify relationships, large firms separate responsibilities for sales (and trade marketing) and consumer marketing. Some firms, e.g. Henkel in Germany, additionally have consumer relations departments that manage the toll-free telephone hotlines found on packaging and generally represent the consumer point of view.

If relationships are paramount, and therefore the focus of planning, the structure of marketing plans should also be relational. That is, rather than follow a 4P structure, as most do, plans should be structured around the brand's key relationships. Since, to our knowledge, no firms take this logic to planning stage, it may be helpful to see what a relational plan would look like – *see* Table 5.2.

**Table 5.2    A relational plan format**

---

Executive summary with planned key profit and brand equity performance indicators versus current and prior year

- Positioning statement as defined above.
- Lessons learned from past, competition, affiliates etc.
- Assumptions (environmental and competition).
- Key players in the brand network, including all key direct customer and end-consumer segments.
- Relationship priorities, i.e. which customer types and segments require, and will repay, most attention.
- Marketing action plan with resource implication (time and money): activities are listed by relationship.
- Relational (brand equity) metrics, i.e. the state of the priority relationships today and how they should be at the end of the planning period.
- Profit and loss account projections versus current and past years.

---

One of the rules of journalism is to write "top down," that is, place paragraphs in declining order of importance so that editors may easily cut paragraphs to fit the space. The same applies to relational plans. List the activities in descending order of importance so that if senior management must prune (it will!), it will cut from the bottom and do least damage to the intentions of the planners.

Marketers have long advocated seeing brands from the consumer's point of view. But traditional planning techniques have focused on the levers the marketer can pull to engineer sales, and profits, growth. Empathy, as the primary marketing tool, has received little attention.

## Internationalizing

International market planning involves two separate, but interwoven, activities: understanding the network of relationships at the national level and integrating local information socially across the entire organization so that its corporate energies can be directed most effectively.

Borders of all kinds obstruct learning. The most obvious are national boundaries. Every country sees itself as different, which it is, but in so doing fails to recognize the similarities – similarities that spell profit. The least obvious boundaries are hierarchical. When a manager takes the plan in for approval, is he looking for some new thinking or a pat on the back? When his boss sees him come in, is he hoping to learn, or to pass on, some hard-won wisdom? Too often, neither is listening nor learning.

In a SILK culture, such as Japan certainly used to be, both senior and junior managers see the discussion of the plan as an opportunity to learn from the other. Thus the approval process is part of the plan formulation. Hierarchic meetings are opportunities for youth to learn from age, and experience to learn what is new. Nonaka and Takeuchi refer to this exchange as "middle-up-down," emphasising the role of middle management in driving this two-way learning process.[13] As a result, the plan is improved consensually.

For "middle management" read "international." The international marketer is outside the national hierarchy and has relationships at several levels. This can work to advantage where there is trust, not least in presenting the potential learning in a non-authoritarian manner. Equally, the border can be aggravated where the international participation is seen as manipulative or political and, of course, international marketers have their own hierarchy to contend with.

Senior manager intervention is partly a matter of timing. Senior management should, as the Irish put it, get its retaliation in first. Expectations and parameters should be set and debated early. Its contribution should be made at the briefing stage. Thereafter, senior management should not interfere. This applies equally to international management. By the time the authoring team has agreed to a plan, further suggestions will be resented, if not rejected.

First or last depends on culture. In the Japanese scenario, last is fine. In Western organizations it may need to be first with plan approval (if the early suggestions have been incorporated) as merely a rubber stamp. Either way, international managers must ensure cross-border learning before plans become formalized. In addition to national and hierarchic borders, time (learning from the past), functional (learning from other specialists within and without the company), customer, and competitor borders may need to be removed. "Borders" here refer to barriers to learning. We are trying to create what Jack Welch called the "Borderless Company."

Most firms have an annual planning cycle with intense activity for the brand – country units at peak times. This presents problems for international managers who cannot be everywhere at once. In practice, this means that the end of the planning season, with its cathartic agreements, is the beginning of the next cross-border learning process after a due interval for players to catch their breath. This, in turn, is why quarterly updates should not be allowed to re-seal their minds. An unending stream of quarterly reaffirmations closes out radical innovation.

# Executive notes

- Both the content and process of planning are the international marketer's primary tools toward performance achievement, a task usually exercised without formal authority. If faced with a choice, the international marketer should be more concerned with enhancing local learning, i.e. process rather than content

- National marketers will do what they are going to do, regardless of a written plan. So the international marketer must first focus on sharing mind-sets – not formal approval

- WEM puts the key process components in the sequence:
  - "War" provides positioning, assumptions about the battleground and how it is changing, and fundamental strategy
  - "Empathy" releases the human characteristics from which new insights flow; and only then
  - "Math" is needed to assess the profitability of the choices made and provide control. If the sophisticated financial analysis does not add up to acceptable performance, another WEM iteration will be required

- Planning should be not only a learning process but also should build the team's commitment to ensure that the planned, or better, performance is delivered. This, in turn, demands motivation with, perhaps, ingredients both from the Coué and Lincoln styles that headed this chapter. Use scenarios to imagine the impossible and then go mad. Have fun. Whether any scenario captures the actual future is beside the point. They develop flexibility

- Firms like General Electric dismantle the arbitrary boundaries between initiatives, training, and planning. Innovations of all kinds, and establishing what effects they would have on the firm's future, should be key to planning teams and not hived off to separate functional silos

- Integrating all forms of futuring (planning, training, task forces) releases time for better plans and better day-to-day management. Modern international groups have more initiatives than they can handle. Empowered middle managers believe initiative creation to be their role but top managers create them too. We are not suggesting a bonfire of initiatives, though that may not be a bad idea, so much as prioritizing and integrating them into planning

# References

1. Inge, C. (1928) "On Monsieur Coué."
2. Letter to General U.S. Grant before Gettysburg.
3. For example, Lysonski, S. and Pecotich, A. (1992) "Strategic Marketing Planning, Environmental Uncertainty and Performance," *International Journal of Research in Marketing*, Vol. 9 pp. 247–255.
4. Aaby, N. and Slater, S. F. (1989) "Management Influences on Export Performance: A review of the empirical literature 1978–1988," *International Marketing Review*, Vol. 6, No. 4, pp. 7–26.
5. Tse-Tung, M. (1967) *Selected Works*. Peking: Foreign Languages Press, Ch. V(1), p. 205.
6. Lee, J. (1997) "Forget research, just come up with a great idea," *The Times*, London, 25 November.
7. Barney, J.B. (1991) "Special Theory Forum – The Resource-Based Model of the Firm: Origins, implications and prospects," *Journal of Management*, 17(1) pp. 97–120.
8. Prahalad, C.K. and Hamel, G. (1990) "The Core Competence of the Corporation," *Harvard Business Review*, May–June, pp. 79–91.
9. Ries, A. and Trout, J. (1986) *Positioning: The battle for your mind*. New York: McGraw-Hill.
10. Reeves, R. (1961) *Reality in Advertising*. New York: Alfred A. Knopf Inc.
11. JELL-O.
12. US positioning for Range Rover, mid-1980s.
13. Nonaka, I. and Takeuchi, H. (1995) *The Knowledge-Creating Company*. Oxford University Press.

# 6

# PASSION

## Creating commitment, purpose and identity

'Tis known by the name of perseverance in a good cause, and of obstinacy in a bad one'

*Source:* L. Sterne[1]

'In pursuit of our everyday tasks and objectives, it is all too easy to forget the less rational and instrumental, the more expressive social tissue around us that gives those tasks meaning'

*Source:* A. M. Pettigrew[2]

Alan Hed's career began at Procter & Gamble (P&G) as part of a sales team in Seattle, Washington in 1983. From there it was on to California and corporate headquarters in Cincinnati. In 1988 he decided he wanted to "go international," and moved to the export sales division in New York, where he was responsible for building businesses in some of the most beautiful locations in the world, including Guam, Samoa, Sipan and Micronesia. He travelled, made friends (mostly with distributors), and sold a great deal of soap powder and Pringles Chips.

In 1990 Alan moved to P&G's export headquarters in Geneva where he became involved in new and emerging Asian markets. When managing the Asia food/beverage business, he had the opportunity to visit Vietnam independently. Although the country was subject to an American trade embargo at the time, Alan wanted to be prepared for the inevitable time when

American corporations would be allowed to do business in this emerging market of 73 million consumers – the eleventh largest population in the world. After just two days in the country, Alan became passionate and asked his management if he could be assigned to work on Vietnam. The company, however, was less enthusiastic, adopting a "wait and see" attitude. But, once the US government lifted sanctions, Alan's perseverance and commitment won through and he was given the job of making something out of Vietnam for the company.

Before taking off for Ho Chi Minh City, Alan voluntarily attended a course in Vietnamese language (60 hours per week for 10 weeks) to allow him to at least communicate at a basic level. Alan decided not to stay in a large international hotel while permanent accommodation was being found. Instead, he found a Vietnamese family to live with so he could learn the culture and continue his language studies. Alan then began creating a business.

By April 1998 P&G had invested over US$80 million in Vietnam and employed over 400 staff, 95 percent of them being locals. This made P&G one of the largest US corporations doing business in Vietnam. Turnover was in excess of US$25 million and P&G was the leader in two out of the three categories in which it competed. But it hadn't been easy. An important part of Alan's success has been his perseverance and personal commitment to both the market and the people with whom he had developed relationships. Vietnam had experienced tremendous growing pains and with that came change, uncertainty and the need to be flexible. During the early years of Vietnam's open door policy (Doi Moi), many companies had come and gone. Led by Alan Hed, P&G has stuck it out. It now believes in the long-term potential of Vietnam and in its ability to succeed in this new market. Alan knows that success is relative – compared with other P&G markets there is room for improvement, but compared with other businesses in Vietnam, P&G is a great success.

---

A few years ago, Donald Clifford and Richard Cavanagh reviewed business success stories in a search for common factors.[3] In almost every case they found "commitment amounting to obsession." As we have discussed, commitment and energy – passion, if you like – are critical in the shift from domestic marketing to exporting. That commitment is based not on quantitative analysis but on instincts, faith and personal vision. Beliefs, not rational planning, make one travel to the action to explore, to risk adversity and vulnerability to alien cultures. These were hallmarks of the Crusaders nearly a millennium ago. Today they are the hallmarks of successful international marketers, such as Alan Hed of Procter & Gamble.

This chapter integrates the three components of a firm's international business success: first, its fundamental purpose; second, the group of non-rational characteristics, such as commitment, obsession, and tenacity, which we collectively call "animal spirits"; and third, information. This blending stands in contrast to the machine models of business that rely on economics and information and which dominated nineteenth and twentieth century analysis. The difference is life itself. What animates a corporation? What drives it?

Relationships, shared information, knowledge and planning, strategy and learning across borders are all necessary. But they are not sufficient. Well-oiled corporate networks and systems are important. But neither are they enough. Take the British civil service, designed for efficiency as the ideal *administrative machine*. Its role was simply to advise politicians and implement their decisions. It is simply a self-perpetuating bureaucracy, which facilitates, but does not drive, political initiatives.

So far as we know, the human is the only animal that self-consciously worries about purpose and identity. City cats, transferred to the country, catch rabbits without lodging fresh strategic plans triggered by the change in the environment. But humans have choices and need to be motivated by a sense of achieving something worthwhile.

*The human is the only animal that self-consciously worries about purpose and identity*

We have seen how relationships provide conduits and how the conversion of implicit experience to explicit knowledge, via Social Information, Learning and Knowledge (SILK), creates value for the firm. Missing, thus far, is the real driver or the corporate life force. There are, of course, vital life forces within each dyad. Like the amber rods in our school physics classes, they all have to be rubbed the same way to create magnetic and electric fields. Without consistent organizational direction, these energies cancel each other out. We need to understand the source of these wilder energies and how they can be made to operate for the benefit of the whole. Ungoverned, they cause mayhem. We are concerned here with the way these dyadic energies come together in totality for the corporation.

So we now extend SILK to the complete PASSION model (Purpose, Animal Spirits, Social Information and Organizational Knowledge), which explains the whole firm's performance. SILK is the last part of that, with the acronym altered to fit its new context. PASSION is the organizational equivalent of the MAC model at the personal level and the sequence is equally important. All three elements, purpose, animal spirits and knowledge matter but purpose comes before animal spirits, which comes before knowledge (SILK). We now consider:

- *Purpose*, which includes corporate identity and the firm's reason for existence)

- *Animal spirits*, the vital force of business success that Keynes could not ascribe to rationality.

# Purpose

Chapter 5 reviewed strategy with intentional brevity. We limited it to its original meaning: planning, acquiring adequate resources and leadership, and merged the first two. Similarly, great swathes of managerial time should not be devoted to formal mission and vision statements. Too often the results are so many well-phrased platitudes. Language becomes illusive; words often disguise more than they reveal. In this section it is easier to review how *not* to deal with purpose before moving to the positive (leadership).

*The Mission Book* contains 301 corporate mission statements from US companies. These statements are remarkably similar. The most popular words were: service (used 230 times), customers (211), quality (194), value (183), employees (157), growth (118), environment (117), profit (114), shareholders (114), leader (104), and best (used 102 times).[4]

The evidence to support clearly-articulated purpose and identity is sparse. The London-based Institute of Personnel and Development undertook an in-depth study of 15 international corporations, including Texas Instruments and Johnson & Johnson. They found that companies *without* mission statements had the more apparent sense of mission.[5]

How is this possible? We refer to the Memory Affect Cognition scheme of comprehension and decision; employees need to *feel* a culture before they *think* it. A sense of shared identity and purpose depends first on Memory and Affect and, only later, the Cognitive workings of the group. Thus it is hardly surprising that analysis destroys the very thing it is trying to analyze.

Take, for example, the corporate video, which usually begins its journey as a cognitive exercise. The script is written, the visuals are added and, finally, the music. The result may be sterile unction that embalms rather than enthuses. One of the authors asked a production company to reverse this process. They were horrified. How could they choose music without knowing what was to be said or filmed? After much debate, it was finally done. The music first provided the desired feeling, or mood, of the company, then the pictures added the visual dimension and brought that music to life, mostly using employees. Finally, the script had to make sense of what was being communicated through music and pictures. The sequence was MAC: empathizing with current employee experience of the corporation (M), using music primarily to shift that toward the desired positioning, i.e. mood and feelings (A), followed by visuals and using only words, to a limited extent, to rationalize and justify the shift (C).

To state that shared purpose frames and gives direction, leading to co-operation rather than conflict, states the obvious. How blatantly transparent, you say! But if relationships, SILK or passion are so vital, let us not dismiss them as obvious. We need new ways to build and measure those characteristics.

## Benchmarking

In building and assessing purpose, the process might begin with identifying relevant high- and low-performing benchmark companies. What did they do? What does it feel like to work for them? What is regarded as "success"? What behavior is penalized? Employees transferred from those companies may be able to bring this exploration to life. The point is not to become a clone of some other organisation, but to learn from its good and bad habits and then incorporate that learning into the firm's own identity. The five big accounting firms have explored what made Arthur Andersen (AA) a high benchmark, stand out from the rest in the eyes of clients. Of particular interest was the perception of a culture at AA that led to employees having an overwhelming sense of self confidence and self belief. The question

# Running to riches

Douglas Spink started Timberline, an endurance sports nutrition website, with $180,000 in 1996. Two years later, aged 27, he sold the business for $5 million to sports retailer G.I. Joe's of Wilsonville, Oregon. Michael Krauss interviewed him to find the roots of his success.

Spink holds an MBA from University of Chicago but rejects the "rational man" of economics. He understands Porter's Five Forces but takes a social perspective: "We contextualize our world through a system of meanings and relationships, systems of social reciprocity, [and] that's what branding is about."

Spink himself lives his customers' lifestyle, uses and believes passionately in his own products. He runs ultra-marathons (more than the marathon distance), climbs rocks, wrestles and rides horses. The original catalogue was extended into snowboarding and duck-hunting products. He is obsessive: "I would make index cards of every item I owned when I was eight years old. Every great brand has an obsessive personality behind it somewhere. Entrepreneurs who succeed use obsessiveness as a tool." As a result he pays huge attention to detail.

He sold out rather than taking the longer road to going public because he loves marketing, not finance. As you might expect, he is action-oriented. But most of all he is passionate. His advice for the new entrepreneur is: "Throw a lot of passion at the wall and see what sticks. In the early days there's more passion than revenue. Over time the revenue starts to backfill the passion."

Source: Krauss M. "David.coms challenge Goliath marketers" and "Entrepreneur goes the distance – and more," Marketing News, 15 March 1999, pp. 7–8

was: "How does that feel and what would we have to do to create that here?"

Adopting examples from others, with appropriate modifications, should lead straight to market actions without dependence upon the well-phrased mission statement. What do all levels of management need to *do* differently? Creating new task forces and lists of values are not what we mean; we are talking about changes that the customer can see, for example, the total re-orientation to customer service by the British Airways staff around 1990. One of the strongest pieces of evidence in the area of purpose and identity is market orientation.[6]

## Profits

Most managers define success in financial terms. The idea that companies are owned by shareholders, and exist for their profit, is deeply embedded, albeit more recently challenged by stakeholder concepts.[7] Charles Handy suggested that making profits for shareholders was more in the nature of hygiene than destination.[8] Ted Levitt also regards profit as a by-product of a company's true purpose. Most of us eat to live rather than live to eat. In the same way, corporations have to ensure that their stakeholders, including the shareholders, are satisfied *in order to* pursue their own goals.

The British inventor, James Dyson, was determined to make a better vacuum cleaner. Financing the invention and then paying dividends to shareholders were necessary but they were not the *goal* of the business. Better vacuum cleaners were. On a bigger scale, Bill Gates and colleagues created Microsoft to meet user needs they empathized with. There was no profit plan.

Adequate shareholder returns, managing a loyal workforce and pleasing customers are universals. Many CEOs have announced these blinding glimpses of the obvious, only to be surprised by the ensuing apathy of employees. No one doubts their importance. But they do not distinguish one company from another. All companies must do these things. The workforce needs a sense of unique purpose and identity: they need to feel different before they can feel special.

## The experiential

Corporate purpose and identity come about more slowly than writing a mission statement, but are more effective. Sensing rarely keeps pace with thinking; it is often a tortoise and hare relationship. We lay stress on the need to build identity experientially and through shared implicit information. Planning for the corporate brand is little different than any other brand: reconnaissance (E+3Cs) should be followed by the positioning statement (purpose) and then corporate brand essence (identity). Test the positioning and essence by replacing the name of the company with a competitor's. Do they still make sense? If so, start again: you have missed. Differentiation remains key – or indeed our own need for self-identity.

Look at the problems encountered when cultures are thrown together. The primary reason for the failure of acquisitions is that these differences have not been understood pre-merger nor managed after the event. Smith Kline Beecham is one of the rare examples of a successful merger. They then pulled back, in 1998, from the later planned merger with Glaxo-Wellcome when it seemed to them that the trick could not be repeated.

Procter & Gamble has a very simple approach to acquisitions – "Procterize" the assets (brands, people etc.) as fast as possible. That which cannot, or will not (in the case of people), be "Procterized" falls by the wayside. The acquisition of Richardson Vicks was a classic example of this philosophy in practice. Another bold approach is to bring two different, but complementary, cultures together, and use the discontinuity created by the merger as an excuse to build a new sense of identity. The "breakaway" program at the newly-formed PricewaterhouseCoopers is an example. Interestingly, the imminent split of Andersen Consulting from parent Arthur Andersen is an example of the reverse – two distinct cultures emerged from one.

## Ethics

Another test of identity is corporate ethics. The modern global corporation tends to create ethical standards distanced from the main business of the company. A committee is charged with their creation and oversight, but what emerges lays the values of one national culture (e.g. the US) on another (e.g. China). This literally is "fascism." Far from helping international managers, they put them under additional stress. This minefield should not delay us beyond noting that ethics should not be separate, but part of the fabric.

In the range of standards from ethical fascism to agnosticism, we veer to less being more, i.e. have few rules but implement them consistently. Those arguing for agnosticism, i.e. pragmatism, argue that international trade is quite difficult enough without unnecessary ethical baggage. On the other side, some companies, e.g. Johnson & Johnson, do well precisely because they have, and live by, high ethical standards. In the business context, a mix of the two, as between different executives, or different times or different countries, is the worst solution. Ethical standards for the firm should be developed *as part of* the firm's purpose and identity.

In the end, the words on paper and in speeches make little difference until they are turned into actions, and especially top management actions. The talk has to be "walked" before it takes effect. One global foods business sent all employees pads of Post-it Notes with the corporate values printed on the cover. One value was tolerance of maverick, or at least free-spirited, management behavior. Everyone knew that, in practice, any expression of independence was severely punished. Conformity continued to rule.

If a unique identity can be achieved, the organization has made a great step: it has captured the "employer brand."[9] Market-oriented companies are more profitable than those that are not.[10] To be competitively oriented is good, but customer orientated is, in general, better. "Oriented" implies "aligned." Today's employees are not building the pyramids but achieving their own satisfactions, just like customers. The company provides the networking, through a belief in the same corporate brand, for employees who feel like customers and customers who feel like family members.

*Buying a chocolate bar is not buying into Hershey's mission and values*

Of course this is stretching the point. Buying a chocolate bar is not buying into Hershey's mission and values. The employee, likewise, is working for money to realize private ambitions. Corporate purpose and identity can make only a limited impact no matter how well they are developed. At the same time, the better they are developed, the more helpful they can be.

So how does a company establish shared purpose? In many ways, we suggest: generally by giving people their brains back, challenging them to take initiatives, developing a learning culture, and distributing leadership. Professor Sumantra Ghoshal and colleagues argue persuasively that we should reject the three Ss (Strategy, Structure and System) in favor of the three Ps: Purpose, Process and People.[11] Purpose cannot be switched on and off, but firms can be more self-aware of why they are different and how they need to be better.

There are two simple measures that can be collected from employees: awareness of, and commitment to, the corporate goals. Weak measures may indicate poor internal marketing but they may equally indicate that the goals are poor, that they lack excitement, motivation and internal cohesion. If nobody salutes when the flag is run up the pole, it may be the wrong flag. Just as when developing any brand essence, the key ingredients are the application of imagination to the realities of the firm's culture.

Cultures are not created by memo and, contrary to today's prescriptions, we doubt the value of *analyzing* values. Culture is created by what management, and especially top management, does, measures and rewards – in that order. Structure, analysis, and dialogue contribute. But experience dominates advertising in organizational culture just as it does in packaged goods marketing. Top management cannot guarantee to make animal spirits or creativity flourish. But it can remove the obstacles. Senior management can create a climate in which creativity *may* flourish. In the same way, you cannot *make* sales but an attractive stall increases the chances.

Ghoshal and colleagues assert, and we agree, that an enabling culture, together with a sense of unique identity and purpose, give direction. Of course, you could call that leadership and you would be right. Leadership lies in communicating purpose in such a way that people are enthused to achieve it, which brings us to animal spirits.

## Animal spirits

In *The New Pioneers*, Petzinger describes the turnaround of Rowe Furniture Co. through the release of creativity and initiative among its plant workers.[12] As the story began, the company found it could not respond quickly to custom orders and badly needed a hyper-efficient assembly process. Taking one look at the plant, the well-experienced manager, Charlene Pedrolie, realized that "the answer to Rowe's problems would never come solely from her. Nor could it come from any one leader. In her view, the answer resided mainly in the collective minds of those doing the work."

First, the workers were removed from operating in separation where each had been confined to specialized tasks. Everyone received a crash course in skills they had seen only from a distance. Paint was scraped from the windows, which had been painted to save on air conditioning. Supervisory positions and entire departments were eliminated.

Before long, 500 workers were assembling themselves into clusters, or "cells." Each group selected its own members and created its own processes and each was given responsibility for a particular product line. Managers, engineers, and technical specialists acted mainly as back-ups, or consultants, leaving the employees to develop the new system on their own.

In addition, Pedrolie installed a "safety net" of information. Each member of every team had instant access to up-to-date information – about order flows, order output, productivity, and quality. Data, once closely guarded by top management, became the common property of the shop floor. People had the instantaneous opportunity to see which of their actions worked and which didn't. They reacted and adjusted their work accordingly.

Of course, there were difficult adjustments, skepticism, and setbacks. There was resistance by stakeholders in the old system. The firm's computer chief had to be ousted. As the pieces slowly fell into place, though, "people unaccustomed to talking with anyone other than the folks at the adjacent station began coursing the four corners of the factory, chatting up anyone who might offer the glimmer of a solution to the problem of the moment ... an informal process of give-and-take emerged between teams as well as within teams."

Once the system was fully installed, the plant was delivering custom-made goods within 30 days – later 10 days – in an industry accustomed to lead times of 6 months. The Rowe Furniture turnaround is meaningful on many levels, writes Petzinger: "It dramatizes the range of initiatives that people display when freed to do their best work. It reveals the creative power of human interaction. It suggests that efficiency is intrinsic; that people are naturally productive; that when inspired with vision, equipped with the right tools, and guided by information about their own performance, people will build on each other's actions to a more efficient result than any single brain could design. In fact it's rather like saying that being good in business calls on being good at being human."

As much as anything, the Rowe Furniture turnaround captures "animal spirits," or spontaneous adaptation, at work. Consider a few telling words and phrases: "collective mind," "cells," "develop the new system on their own," "build on each other's actions." Are we not describing this collective as an organism?

Planning, structure, command and control work when all the critical elements of a system are understood. In a competitive environment of rapid product cycle times and unpredictable consumers, control may be illusory. In the global economy, the corporation is no longer a discrete entity: it dwells within a complex ecosystem and cannot live in isolation. The innovations of people such as Alan Hed and Douglas Spink illustrate the place of "animal spirits" as a unifier, accommodating these realities.

If we then choose to perceive the organization as an organism that lives within ecosystems, we must allow for the principle of emergence and, in addition, complexity, the foil of planning.

When systems become sufficiently complex and interconnected, the interaction self-assembles into a new, higher order: molecules into cells, cells into organs, organs into organisms, organisms into societies. This is natural economizing, life creating more from less, something from nothing. At each level, emergence creates more than the sum of its parts. The strength of an alloy may exceed the combined strength of the metals that compose it. A jazz ensemble creates a sound that no one could imagine by listening to the instruments individually. What appears chaotic at one level (the bustle of a million computer users) may generate stunningly ordered behavior at the next level (a new medium called the Internet). None of this can be predicted or controlled.

The question is, what drives this process? The life force is little enough understood in biology to attempt a full answer in the organizational equivalent. We can recognize its vigour in adolescents and its embers in the aged but we do not understand why. There are some differences in companies: they do not have to die and they can be rejuvenated. A few survive for centuries.

Arie de Geus has explained part of this. Firms adapt by constantly experimenting at their borders. He does not, however, explain what the life force is and nor can we. What has been done, however, is to see what leaders do.

Charles Farkas, Philippe de Backer and Allen Sheppard, for example, asked 160 successful chairmen and CEOs how they did it.[13] The first lesson is that there are many successful styles. Some leaders are reclusive and some are extraverted. Some say little and some are rarely off a platform.

> *Firms adapt by constantly experimenting at their borders*

The moral is that you do not judge the quality of conductors by watching what they do on the podium, but by observing the effect on the orchestra. The quality of a leader can be estimated, even quantified, by the employees' clarity of understanding of, and commitment to, purpose and the increase in animal spirits generated. A battery of indicators – from enthusiasm to energy, to tenacity to certainty and courage – will be needed for that.

Some things are near-universal, whether for conductors or business leaders. They empathize, they listen, they see for themselves and they communicate effectively. They are not just facilitators, though modern leadership thinking seems to be drifting that way, because they should be driving, not driven by, their own people.[14] While a leader conveys purpose and vision, he is not necessarily being a "visionary." Independent sensing, thinking, and judgment are all necessary but that does not preclude fostering the ideas of others. Indeed the reverse is true. Nothing motivates a management team more than knowing that they will not only be heard but that their contributions will be implemented. Those liberated "animals" in a PASSION system may create a far more compelling vision than one leader alone may contrive.

There is no formula; if anything, the better leaders are those who listen to their instincts and direct their activities according to the needs of their divisions, their companies and the environment in which they are presented. They are comfortable within a MAC sequence of decision making and create an environment that fosters free-flowing dialogue, where playfulness is considered a lubricant of imagination, where paradox is not feared.

*The better leaders are those who listen to their instincts*

The practical CEO will be conscious of the need to grow vitality, animal spirits. As a precursor to profits and shareholder value, vitality is far more important. He can measure whether his *modus operandi* is having that effect and, if it is not, what he has to change. For it is this, purpose and animal spirits, that is the leader's main job.

## The PASSION model

Successful firms exhibit similar characteristics irrespective of national culture. One study across the US, England, France, Germany and Japan reported performance to be affected by:[15]

- Organizational climates that fostered trust, participation, entrepreneurial behavior and flexibility
- External (market) orientation.

We go further and suggest that successful firms universally have:

- **P**urpose and identity
- **A**nimal **S**pirits, the life force and also the emotional aspects of the corporate mind
- Effective ways of sharing **S**ocial **I**nformation
- Creating value through shared learning, i.e. by turning **S**ocial **I**nformation into **O**rganizational k**N**owledge.

The acronym has meaning: passion brings the networks to life and life to the networks. Figure 6.1 integrates these components.

Behavior is nourished by animal spirits, purpose (focus) and knowledge, within the context of the competitive environment. If these elements are weak, the changing environment and competition may induce reactive behavior. If they are strong, however, they use the context to shape new behavior just ahead of when it is needed. Performance outcomes result from behavior, again in the context of environment and competition. Finally, performance outcomes feed back to reinvigorate animal spirits and provide fresh inputs for social information.

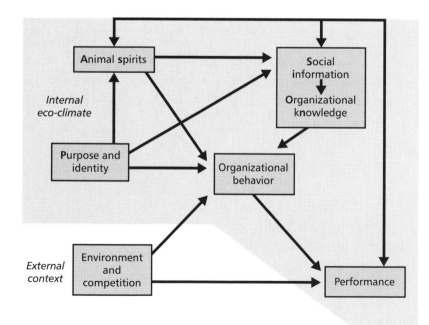

**Fig. 6.1   PASSION**

Like any model of business, PASSION ruthlessly selects only a few key issues for attention. Simplicity is a strength and a danger. The test of a business model is not what has been omitted, but whether it is useful. PASSION is consistent both with science and business observation and literature. The two most empirically grounded books in this area, *Built to Last* and *Corporate Culture and Performance*, bear out this purposive, incremental, biological model as distinct from short-term pre-occupation with shareholder value or mechanical systems.[16]

## Creating the corporate eco-climate

Like other organisms, businesses develop their capabilities without giving them active thought. They grow by default as much as by intent. In today's global competitive arena, however, doing what comes naturally will not be enough. Top management must actively manage corporate culture.

For a start, top management needs to shift its gaze from the bottom line to the top, from profits to customer relationships, from trailing to leading indicators and from results to animal spirits. These shifts are all manifestations of the same thing. Figure 6.1 symbolizes this, placing performance at the bottom and animal spirits and social information at the top. Most firms reward good results, but the difference in cultures, between those penalizing failure and those rewarding trial, is considerable. At the same time, experimenting without making use of existing organizational knowledge, or without sharing the results, is remiss indeed.

*Analyzing what a horse leaves on the road may be an excellent guide to the health of the horse, but it does not tell you where it is going*

The reason for top-line attention is partly that senior management needs to address the business success for the future, not simply study the results of the past. Analyzing what a horse, leaves on the road may be an excellent guide to the health of the horse, but it does not tell you where it is going. Control through financial performance is not the role of the leader, but that of the auditor, i.e. someone who arrives after the battle, counts the dead and bayonets the wounded.

When August Busch III tastes Budweiser in the laboratories in St Louis, he does so from the consumer's point of view, not because that is his job as

CEO but because his attention is symbolic for the rest of his organisation. CEOs of international retailers visit their stores not so much to learn, though that is part of SILK, as to direct attention to corporate purpose. These chief executives are providing the climate for learning across borders.

Managing the climate for knowledge creation, or the process of adaptation to changing environments, can be seen as the ultimate function of a global firm's headquarters. Corporate HQ should provide the overall operating environment for middle managers: experience (corporate memories), culture (corporate feelings) and the sharing of SILK for global benefit.

Some believe that "harmonization" is a euphemism for central control. Most often, the firm's culture and processes evolve without conscious management. Studies of long-lasting companies show that successful firms steer a middle course between standardization and a free-for-all, or between excessive control and none.[17] Clearly, standardization reduces the scope for experimentation. The boundary units of an organism need the freedom to fail and to put out feelers to discover where profitable growth lies. The firm's evolution relies on it adapting to its changing environment. This is largely a process of trial and error.

*Communications come to resemble the Tower of Babel in which everyone talks and no one listens*

On the other hand, a free-for-all also prevents learning from those experiences. The discoveries by one part of the organism are not transmitted successfully to another. Each unit goes its separate way. Communications come to resemble the Tower of Babel in which everyone talks and no one listens.

A variety of local experiences and experimentation is important for learning, not just locally but also for other markets. SILK compares experience across borders through shared frameworks, language and non-verbal communications (culture). Setting implicit upper and lower limits for control and innovation, harmony and experimentation, may be seen as the province of top management. International marketing, in this perspective, takes place *within* those guidelines.

To be able to learn from other markets, comparisons have to be made. This, in turn, requires shared language and measurement systems. Internal boundaries (between business units, countries and functions) need to be at least translucent for the commonwealth of knowledge to be shared.

At the heart of this chapter, indeed, this book, lies the concept of animal spirits: the liberator of vitality, motivation, and commitment, the wellspring of passion. When someone is sick or very tired, they can, at best, only maintain themselves. Mere survival is all they can achieve. So it is with corporations. Those that are just (pre-occupied with) surviving are dangerously low on healthy animal spirits. Finding the right medicine is no easy matter. Re-engineering and shareholder-value consultants recommend blood letting and/or amputation. This may be necessary, but it is no cure. It is like the millipede whose doctor suggested that with so many legs performance would be enhanced if the least productive were amputated. After a few visits, the one-time-millipede hopped in sorely troubled. The doctor gave it a large brandy: "A cure? Of course not. You're so far gone you may as well be legless." The British textiles firm, Courtaulds, went from leadership to demise following this path.

As shown in the Rowe Furniture story, amputation is sometimes necessary to remove gangrenous corporate body parts. But surgery does not create vitality. Indeed, for major surgery to work, the patient needs a strong life force to withstand the shock. The same is true of all living things. The most frequent, and most successful, approach is to introduce a high octane executive, such as Lou Gerstner, into IBM with enough energy, enthusiasm, and authority to enliven everyone else. For example, Bill Gates' *Win2000* product had, by December 1998, 30 million program lines and was quietly imploding. A new project leader was appointed. He summoned the entire 3,000-strong team to the canteen, gave them a simple set of priorities, and rekindled enthusiasm. Many volunteered to work over the holiday break. The moral of this story is not that it was a great canteen speech. It may or may not have been. Assembled in that room was an energetic bunch of people desperately seeking new belief. It did not take much.

Look again at the examples of Alan Hed of Procter & Gamble and Douglas Spink of Timberline. What stands out is a passion, a commitment, a dedication bordering on obsession with purpose and goals. There is no confused identity. "We contextualize our world through a system of meanings and relationships, systems of social reciprocity," said Spink.

We suggest two traits: first, strong leaders *develop their people* and facilitate their learning; second, they *trust* in the creative power of human interaction when people are equipped with the right tools, guided by information, and freed to do their best work.

In freeing people to do that work, let us consider that most precious of commodities: time. A distinction between leaders and managers is that leaders *release* time for people to develop their contributions. Great conductors, for example, never waste the time of their players. Sir Simon Marks, chairman of Marks & Spencer in 1956, got down to store level and terminated most of the paperwork – 120 tons of it.[17] Managers, on the other hand, find things for their people to do, notably meetings, and thereby *reduce* their quality time.

Business life is divided into quality time, hygiene time, and wasted time. Quality time is what makes a real difference. Empathizing with customers or making substantive product improvements requires large chunks of time, much of which may seem to be low-level use of great talents but, in aggregate, produces proud results, like playing with your children. Quality time is whatever it takes to be effective, i.e. delivering corporate goals. Marketers today get less quality time than their predecessors. Hygiene time takes two forms: co-operating with colleagues so that they can be effective (otherwise they won't co-operate with you) and checking that money is being used efficiently (planning and performance monitoring). Bottom-line fetishists misunderstand the second of those. Cleanliness is all very well but non-stop bathing suggests a visit to the shrink. Every other use of time is a waste.

This time enlargement perspective of leadership reminds us that leadership does not apply just at the CEO level. Every international manager is, or should be, a leader. Leaders operate within organizational frameworks as well as outside them. Leadership is hard, to teach but it can be learned, especially when a firm sets out to ensure that it is. The PASSION cycle is self-perpetuating.

Measuring the components of the PASSION model, a "PASSION-OMETER" perhaps, is a formidable, but not insurmountable, task. At the simplest level, employee surveys may be conducted annually or every three years. Just as brand equity is monitored using a battery of vital signs, so indicators of PASSION should be developed as part of monitoring corporate health. And CEOs should write single-page statements describing the state of the business in PASSION terms to set beside their accounts. Without knowing if the firm biologically thrives or declines, their accounts will be giving an incomplete picture. PASSION needs to be cherished.

# Executive notes

- Corporate purpose should be derived briefly not as a wish list, but from the firm's real experience. Test and verify it by employees' awareness and commitment to it. Then refine it annually and re-communicate, but not excessively. Test what people feel and do, not what they read

- Develop corporate purpose throughout the whole company with the positioning techniques of Chapter 5

- Leadership, like any other biological trait, is both nature and nurture. Look closely at leadership ratings of all international managers up to and including the CEO. Are they developing shared corporate purpose, animal spirits and growing their people through better use of time?

- Create a "PASSIONOMETER" so that the firm can monitor its corporate health

- Reward experimentation, provided the results are shared. Celebrate small failures to create great successes

- Encourage the implicit social information that leads to learning and organizational knowledge

- Walk the talk. Maintain consistency, which includes holding on to the ethical standards management has determined

# References

1. Sterne, L. *Tristram Shandy*, Ch. 17.
2. Pettigrew, A. M. (1979) "On Studying Organizational Cultures," *Administrative Science Quarterly*, 24, pp. 570–581.
3. Clifford, D. K. Jr and Cavanagh, R. E. (1985) *Winning Performance*, p. 230. New York: Bantam Books.
4. Reported in "Was there life before mission statements?," *Marketing* (UK), 10 July 1997, p. 5.
5. Reported in "Do you really need a mission statement?," *Across the Board*, 32 (7), July/August 1995, pp. 16–20.
6. Meehan, S. A. (1997) "Market Orientation: Values, behaviours and performance." University of London: unpublished PhD dissertation.
   Narver, J. C. and Slater, S. F. (1990) "The Effect of a Market Orientation on Business Profitability," *Journal of Marketing* 54, October, pp. 20–35.
   Slater, S. F. and Narver, J. C. (1994) "Market Orientation, Customer Value, and Superior Performance," *Business Horizons* 37, 2 March/April, pp. 22–28.
   Slater, S. F. and Narver, J. C. (1994) "Does Competitive Environment Moderate the Market Orientation-Performance Relationship?," *Journal of Marketing* 58, January, pp. 46–55.
7. Ambler, T. and Wilson, A. (1995) "The Problems of Stakeholder Theory," *Business Ethics* 4 (1): 30–35.
8. Handy, C. (1991) "What is a Company For?", *RSA Journal*, March.
9. Ambler, T. and Barrow, S. (1996) "The Employer Brand," *The Journal of Brand Management* 4, (3 December), 185–206.
10. Meehan, S. A.; Narver, J. C. and Slater, S. F.; Slater, S. F. and Narver, J. C.; Slater, S. F. and Narver, J. C.; *op. cit.*
11. Ghoshal, S., Bartlett, C. and Moran, P. (1999) "A New Manifesto for Management," *Sloan Management Review*, 40(1), pp. 9–20.
12. Petzinger, T. Jr. (1999) *The New Pioneers: The men and women who are transforming the workplace and marketplace.* New York: Simon & Schuster.
13. Farkas, C. *et al.* (1995) *Maximum Leadership.* London: Orion Books.
14. Bennis, W. G. (1998) *Managing People is like Herding Cats.* London: Kogan Page.
15. Deshpandé, R. *et al.* (1997) *Factors Affecting Organisational Performance: A Five-country Comparison.* Cambridge, Massachussetts: Marketing Science Institute Working Paper, #97–108.
16. For example, de Geus, *The Living Company*, op.cit.
   Kotter, J. and Heskett, J. (1992) *Corporate Culture and Performance.* New York: The Free Press.
   Collins, J. C. and Porras, J. I. (1994) *Built to Last: Successful habits of visionary companies.* New York: Harper Collins.
17. The *Guardian*, 16 May 1960.

# part
# III

# Principles in practice

We have been teaching the material in this book for about five years to executives and students in the US and Australia, China and the UK – not to mention other countries. A regular question is whether these guidelines are just another bunch of ideas, like TQM and re-engineering, which will move along and be replaced. How transitory are these concepts?

Some components are bound to be matters of fashion but the shift from the mechanistic view of business to the biological is fundamental. Taylorism ushered in the twentieth century and the biological view is beginning to flower at the dawn of the twenty-first. Nothing is forever but these principles have a shelf life, we expect, of at least 100 years. The period where reason has been seen to be mankind's distinguishing characteristic has lasted 300 years. As the next chapter suggests, the computer, more logical than us, is changing all that, but at this level of profundity, the change will be slow and long lasting. Furthermore, the glorification of reason is a Western, not an Eastern, tradition. Descartes never influenced Asia, which has always held a more balanced view of the most advanced aspects of humanity.

This prompts an illustration from China. *Guanxi* (relationships) has long been recognized there as the central principle of marketing. The word is new (twentieth century), but the concept is old. Some commentators, e.g. Lee Kuan Yew of Singapore, have observed that *guanxi* substitutes for commercial law, which is undeveloped in China not because they are backward, but because they have not needed it. New idea? Here is a senior British diplomat writing about his observations of doing business in China over 200 years ago:

"The natural sentiments with respect to age, united with affections to kindred, early taking root, and strengthened by a daily sense of services received, often bind the mind more effectually, though with gentle ties, than the force of compulsory laws."[1]

So we are confident that these principles will change as we learn more and they are developed. The basics, however, will be with us for a long time to come.

---

1. Sir George Stauton (1797), *Lord Macartney's Embassy to China*, London: W. Bulmer & Co, p. 301

# International marketing metrics
## Measuring what matters

'Our dilemma is that while we can measure the immediate profit flow from a brand, it is difficult to establish whether we are truly increasing its capacity for producing long-term profits or merely harvesting the fruits of our predecessors'

*Source:* Lord Sheppard of Didgemere, then CEO of Grand Metropolitan PLC[1]

Anglia Direct (name changed), a mail order, consumer goods business based in Norwich, England, started in the first Thatcher boom of the 1980s. During these years the business grew steadily and made a few acquisitions, but debt also grew and bottom-line growth was only enough to satisfy the bank. By 1991, the business was medium sized (about 70 staff) and the founders (previous buyers in a department store) decided to hire professional marketing help to accelerate growth; 1992 saw the implementation of the first plan of the newly recruited marketing manager (consumer-packaged-goods experienced, 30 years old). Unfortunately, sales and margins fell. Anglia Direct reported its first loss since its start-up year. In December 1992, the marketing manager was sacked and all marketing expenditure for 1993 cancelled. Then, as it turned out, 1993 sales, margins, and profits were all at record levels.

Were the owners of Anglia Direct right to sack the marketing manager? As it happened, 1992 was a terrible year for the whole of that business sector, whereas the economy improved in 1993 and, with it, sales and margins for all their competitors too. Even from the limited information provided by this case, it is clear the firm had no means of appraising and separating its brand equity. Even as the company reaped the benefits of its 1992 actions, canceling marketing investments lost the momentum in building brand equity.

The role of marketing as brand building is central. Brand equity is the storehouse of future value and an international marketer is only as good as the brand equity he builds. Of course, the international marketer needs other types of information too: the progress of manufacturing and distribution, payments and inventories, advertising and promotional decisions, to name but a few. Nevertheless, the health of his brand(s) is the primary consideration and metrics are crucial in appraising brand equity.

In this chapter we shift gears, adapting the abstract concepts in our theoretical models (MAC, SILK, WEM, and PASSION) to the practical metrics for the international marketer to improve performance, share learning across borders, and ensure controls are in place. While these models initially may seem confusing, each follows a similar pattern: order emerging from chaos via emotions and feelings.

*The role of marketing as brand building is central*

Now we apply those models, and especially PASSION, initially by selecting measures, then, in the next chapter, by reviewing the main problem of international business, "Not Invented Here" (NIH), and, finally, whether sector-to-sector differences profoundly change management implications.

Measuring marketing performance is important for four main reasons:

- *Improving performance.* Quantifying objectives, realistic staging posts and the costs of reaching them are the crucial latter parts of the WEM (War → Empathy → Math) planning cycle. Evidence suggests that what firms measure is, most often, what they get – especially if it is also what they reward.[2]

- *Learning.* Across units and national boundaries by providing comparisons. While performance improvement applies in any business, cross-border comparisons provide the unique strength of international businesses. Some organizations simply impose standards and thereby learn very little. Approached in a spirit of experiment and inquiry, however, the whole company can gain from the measured experiences of a few.

- *Control.* The steady application of *consistent* measures from objective setting through functional and national plans, implementation and reporting results provides feedback to business managers at all levels. Fascists believe that the more painful the feedback, the more effective the learning. Liberals believe that feedback should be private and gentle to ensure that learning is encouraged.

- *Symbolism.* Perhaps the most important. Measurements inform the whole staff about what top management believes really matters. Thus metrics reinforce leadership.

The essence of our prescription is that primary attention be given to the top (PASSION) line without losing sight of the bottom (performance). In theory, the top, in particular animal spirits, should not be associated just with measurement but should actively drive measurement, albeit in the context of the environment and competition.

We therefore address measurement issues as follows:

- Corporate health. Measures of PASSION
- Performance metrics
- Harmonizing metrics internationally.

## Corporate health

Since the PASSION model is new, there are no time-tested scales that assess the whole picture. Nevertheless, firms should develop their own scales incrementally from pieces already in place. Firms with mission statements routinely test staff recognition and awareness of the mission. We suggest that firms should develop formal positioning (purpose) identity statements for their corporate brands and then test them with their own staff in exactly the same way as conventional brands are tested with consumers. In so doing, test the full Memory Affect Cognition (MAC) sequence. The staff's experience with, and commitment to, the corporate brand are more important than cognitive factors, e.g. awareness.

Measuring animal spirits is not quite the virgin territory it may seem.

Commitment, for example, has long been measured. We suggest the following procedure:

- Identify a number of companies, well-known to the task force, to benchmark the firm's own measurement system.

- Rate these companies overall on a 1–9 scale for animal spirits. Those who ask "exactly what do you mean?" should be given a broad definition, such as that in Chapter 6, but nothing specific. Corporate vitality is easier to identify as a whole than in parts.

- Debate the different opinions and the diversity of the characteristics of corporate vitality. The debate is not to secure consensus, but to secure ways to see animal spirits. Note that we are not deconstructing them into components or dimensions: we are finding different perspectives on the whole.

- These perspectives provide scales for rating your own company's animal spirits.

Finally, we have the SILK (or "SION") parts of the model. It has become fashionable to appoint chief knowledge officers; with that should come some measurement of organizational knowledge, or at least the explicit or digitalized knowledge with which most of these appointments seem primarily concerned. A more formalized approach to data warehousing and internal electronic messaging is to be welcomed but it is not the value-creating part of SILK.

Whatever knowledge measures are being employed, some scales to test SI (Social Information) will be needed. Any old social information is not beneficial. Nothing will be gained from aimless chatting. Our own limited research shows that we should measure only purposive, focused SI.

We accept that measuring PASSION is, at this state of the art, rudimentary. It is nevertheless important because:

- It gets the topic into mainstream top management thinking.
- The search for improved measures will itself improve understanding.
- PASSION matters and finding ways to monitor it brings the model into management thinking.

# Performance

Comparing profits with costs and management efforts requires us to divide performance into neat annual bundles. If, as Lord Sheppard pointed out, we do not account for the state of our marketing assets at the beginning and end of each accounting period, we are confusing this period's performance with the past and the future. The tool we need is brand equity (the marketing asset), which needs to be distinguished from brand valuation (the financial worth of that asset). Just as we match the cost of goods sold with actual sales by using an asset called "stock" or "inventory," so brand equity is the stock-pile of unused marketing effects. To assess marketing performance, we must take into account the change in the size of that stock. Thus performance equals short-term results plus the increase (or decrease) in brand equity.

## Brand equity

Brand equity is, mostly, what people carry around in their heads about the brand.[3] More formally, brand equity is *a set of memories in the extended minds of a brand's customers, channel members, parent corporation, and other key members of its network that will impact future cash flow and profitability.* Memory is used here in the sense of both "procedural" (what we have learned about how to do things, habits and behaviors) and "declarative" (things we remember) memory.[4] The brand as a living being is also a handy metaphor: they are born (launched), need sustenance and die if they are starved or maltreated.

Companies that do not regard themselves as being in the brands' business, e.g. industrial capital goods, should still adopt "brand equity" as the generic term for the marketing asset. They may prefer something like "reputation" or "goodwill," but brand equity is well defined and the most widely-used term.

In the brand equity definition above, "extended minds" refers both to non-brain parts of the body (hormonal conditioning and somatic memory) and to computerized extensions of our memory capacity. When the liquor store clerk presses the re-order vodka button on the computer and an order for Smirnoff arrives automatically with the supplier, that computer programming is part of Smirnoff's brand equity, i.e. a memory has generated cash flow.

The "other network members" refers to influence agents outside traditional distribution channels. For example, a key component of Crest toothpaste's platform, developed in the US, was the endorsement given by the American Dental Association (ADA), making the ADA/Crest relationship important for the brand. A weakening, or less positive, set of memories on the part of the ADA would significantly harm the Crest brand, resulting in, for example, a withdrawal of their endorsement.

Brand equity is not built by ephemeral sales promotions run today and forgotten tomorrow. It is long-term memory, which influences buying and usage behavior. Brand-related memories are not always positive. Perrier took a long time to recover from the benzene adulteration and, perhaps, it never will. These are rare events. More usually a bad service experience, poor product performance, or perhaps an out-of-stock problem may serve to reduce the "net positive" store of brand memories for that consumer. In brief:

- A brand is the inclusive combination of product, packaging, identification and added values.
- If "brand" is used broadly, brand equity is the appropriate label for the firm's intangible asset, created by its marketing activities.
- "Brand equity" is the term for that asset most used by practitioners
- Brand equity is mostly what people remember about the brand.
- The financial or any other *measure* of brand equity, e.g. market share, should be distinguished from the asset itself. Brand valuation is, therefore, one of many useful measures of brand equity, but no more than that.

## Performance metrics[5]

There are four kinds of marketing performance measures:

- *Metrics*, which are the key top-level indicators and should be reviewed with international and senior management.
- *Diagnostics*, which are analyses normally reviewed by the relevant national managers. Diagnostics explain the variances in metrics. Sales turnover, for example, is a metric, but the sales analyses across segments, types of trade customer, and geographic regions, are diagnostics. Similarly, measures of

the performance of individual parts of the marketing mix, such as advertising, are diagnostics, not metrics.

- *Trends* (technically "derivatives"), which show the year-on-year changes in metrics (e.g. sales this year as a percent of last year). Second order, or double, derivatives give us the rate of change, i.e. whether the change is accelerating or slowing down.

- *Other performance measures*, used on special, non-routine occasions, or that co-vary with metrics and diagnostics. They do not need to be reviewed separately.

Since we are dealing with the international big picture, secondary measures, while important, will not be reviewed further, beyond noting that harmonizing metrics implies similar attention to diagnostics in order to understand differences across borders. This is the subject of the next section.

The word "metric" comes from music and verse, and means the underlying rhythm, or measure that consistently repeats. In marketing, a metric is a measure that is both precise and consistent:

- Between marketers
- From accounting period to period
- With finance and accounting measures
- With other marketing metrics, e.g. the same "market" is used in measuring market share and relative price
- And understood across functions, especially finance and accounting.

Examples include market share, relative price, share of voice, brand loyalty, and penetration. Metrics are often ratios and indicate progress towards objectives. As these differ from firm to firm, so will the selected metrics. As such they always concern effectiveness, not necessarily efficiency. Ideally, a firm's set of marketing metrics are:

- Sufficient, i.e. they are comprehensive
- Synchronized with the firm's objectives
- Necessary, i.e. there is minimal internal redundancy of measurement
- Sensitive, i.e. they vary but not excessively
- Predictive, i.e. they indicate future short-term performance as well as performance to date.

There are three types of metrics: short-term performance, waste and brand equity, though few firms actively measure waste. For example, when a promotion is completed, one can tally unused material (delivered too late) and what the promotion should have cost. A list of the 53 most popular metrics are shown in Table 7.2 at the end of this chapter.

Waste needs to be recognized, but attempts to eliminate it are naive. A brand or, more correctly, brand equity, exists as a living entity. As such, it requires regular and consistent nourishment, typically through advertising. This creates waste as all living things do. Brand equity lives in the minds of its customers; firms should be cautious in making that a primary target for savings. Waste can only be stopped by death.

*Brand equity lives in the minds of its customers*

If we could directly measure memory by looking inside people's heads, we could accurately measure brand equity. We must instead settle for performance metrics of six kinds:

- "Direct" measures based on what people *say* they have in their heads. We call these "intermediate" effects as they have yet to change behavior
- Indirect measures based on consumer behavior
- Trade customer or other channel measures. This may include key influencers, such as journalists outside the channels
- Other competitive measures
- Innovation because we know brands die without it
- Other financial indicators of brand strength.

These groups of measures do overlap. We know that affect dominates cognition and that it is disrupted by being tested cognitively. Much brand memory, e.g. habits, are non-conscious. Brand equity measurement aims to use a variety of not unrelated measures (metrics), which provides a fuzzy impression of the asset. It is the best we can do.

Table 7.2 shows some conventional brand equity metrics divided into the categories above. Though far from comprehensive, this is a long list – too long for a single firm's management to handle.[6] Even so, our list is only one-third of the number of metrics that a Swedish financial services firm, Skandia, has been tracking to identify its key marketing indicators. Our metrics are not listed in order of importance, only categorized. We will describe later the empirical process of getting from a long to a manageable list.

In order to keep the list to just over 50 metrics, we have eliminated measures that we consider not to be marketing metrics:

- Trends (derivatives). Growth figures, year-to-year and plan comparisons. All metrics are tracked to provide dynamic comparisons and that takes care of trend presentation.

- Varying periods. Year-to-date, moving annual totals and quarterly and monthly metrics are usual cycles as well as specific pre- and post-campaigns.

- Ratios of two existing metrics. We exclude the third where a calculation can be made from two, even though the third may be widely used, e.g. we have turnover and market share (value) and therefore not total market value.

- Diagnostics, i.e. analyses of metrics by segment, by distribution channel, by sub-brand, or by any particular part of the mix, e.g. awareness of the advertising. Diagnostics are used by *middle* managers (marketers) to explain variances in metrics.

We are not suggesting management ignore these other measures. First- and second-order derivatives (trends and the rates of change of trends), for example, are very important and will need to be included if the presentation of the metrics themselves does not convey the dynamic picture.

There are two approaches to reducing a list of metrics to the length top management can handle (one page): theoretical and pragmatic. Both are needed, but let us start with the theory. Brand equity comprises the brand memories of those who form the brand's relational network: consumers, channel members, the sales force and so on. Relational measures of brand equity can be constructed using a four-step process:[7]

*Step 1: Determine which relationships are key.* Depending on the market, the environment and the development of the firm/brand, consumers (perhaps different segments), distributors (wholesalers, retailers, agents), suppliers (e.g. Intel for PC suppliers, Nutrasweet for Diet Coke/Pepsi) or opinion leaders (e.g. medical practitioners in pharmaceutical categories, sections of the media) may be the gateway to success. End users matter in the long run but the immediate customer matters first. The relationship between the brand and the sales force matters even sooner, especially with a multi-brand portfolio, as in the case of Procter & Gamble.

*Step 2: Identify the major factors in each relationship.* What drives the formation, development and maintenance of the key relationships? As we saw in Chapter 2, relationships pass through a series of stages: i) awareness, ii) exploration, iii) expansion, iv) commitment, v) dissolution.[8] Each relevant variable can be measured, e.g. awareness – recall/recognition; expansion – trust and satisfaction. Cases have been made for perceived quality (esteem) and brand commitment as the most predictive measures of future share gains and, no doubt, cases for other variables will also be made. Market research, past experience and judgment can help determine which indicators are most appropriate for each brand/market/environment. Until they have been empirically verified, they should have the benefit of the doubt.

*Step 3: Develop relationship measurement scales.* Relationship measurement is still in its infancy. A 1998 textbook on business relationship marketing did not deal with measurement at all.[9] Some relationship indicators are already in common use, e.g. recall/recognition. Others, such as commitment and trust, have been developed and used in both commercial and academic research. Relational measures still need to be adapted and tested for reliability and validity in different settings. Does that mean we should be reviewing trends (derivatives) not metrics? Not necessarily. We are comparing the state of the asset (brand equity) at two points in time. You *may* need derivatives to measure the asset, but metrics should suffice.

*Step 4: Identify the measures that matter and track them regularly.* Not all measures will be useful. Those that are sensitive and shown to be linked to cash flow in the past are those that should be included in the final Brand Equity Monitor (see discussion below). Furthermore, one-off measurement does not tell managers the real state of the brand, e.g. in decline or improving. Brand equity is a dynamic phenomenon. As stressed earlier, it is *changes* in brand equity, not the absolute values, that matter.

While this is an important mental process to follow, some key metrics will not be available and others will not perform as they should. The pragmatic approach is to throw all likely metrics and derivatives, starting with those in Table 7.2, in a hopper and then use the ones that seem to work, i.e. fitting the above specification of being sensitive and predictive.

Debate between international and local marketers on how brand equity should be tracked will yield a rich assortment of points of view which, for a happy change, do not need to be argued out. Using back-data so far as it is available, try all the measures that attract worthwhile managerial support. Be inclusive at this stage. From whatever sources, a long list of potential brand equity metrics and derivatives, perhaps 100, will emerge. That can be reduced to a manageable list (10–20) in two stages: debate between experienced marketers and IT analysis. Some will duplicate each other (co-vary), some will be over-sensitive (bounce around too much) and others too insensitive. Others will simply not apply to that sector. Packaged-goods marketers, for example, measure the penetration of mass markets whereas financial services count their actual customers. Some segment customers into those they really care about and pay little attention to other segments. A day's discussion should prune the list (perhaps adding a few) to the point where quantification is necessary (perhaps 20–30).

The state of brand equity at any point in time is less important than the *change*, and especially the *direction of change*, from the beginning to the end of the period of assessment. Measures that do not change do not help.

All remaining potential metrics should be modeled for their predictiveness of future performance using historical data. What happened earlier does not dictate the future, but it should illuminate at least *did* metrics that work. The choices that management now makes should be maintained for many years. Transitioning from an old to a new set of metrics is a long, complex and expensive business, if done properly.

Applying both theory and practice, the resulting metrics (and derivatives) should be:

- *Precise and sensitive*. Trends over long periods are still more valuable.

- *Predictive*. Measuring brand equity should indicate what, other things being equal, the future holds. We cannot measure the future, only the past. Brand equity is today's storehouse of tomorrow's profits.

- *Reliable*. False correlations, between share and profit, for example, create false trails.

- *Relevant*. Describing the essence of the brand. If the essence of Avis is trying harder, then service performance measures need to capture the customers' perception of whether Avis staff are trying. If fashionability is irrelevant to the Avis brand, then do not let the new Parisian product manager, or the new Indian research company, insist on fashionability indices. You will be tempted to let them make a purely local, additional measure, but don't do it. Measures beget actions and brand essence will be compromised.

- *Economical.* In a *stable* market, most of the time, market shares predict loyalty, penetration, distribution and many other traditional brand equity measures, but then in a stable market not much is changing anyway. Marketers, however, are interested in what causes markets to *destabilize*, not their inherent consistency; they are looking for exceptions, not rules. Nevertheless, marketers should be interested in reducing the number of measures.

Biology tells us that nature deliberately leaves waste because today's fat is tomorrow's survival. Experimentation and evolution necessarily create redundancy. Some metrics are inherently redundant because they are mathematically related (two measures and their ratio, for example) but some independent measures that *should* be important, even though they seem not to be functioning, ought to be kept. Measures that failed to predict performance in 2000, may do so two years later.

*Nature deliberately leaves waste because today's fat is tomorrow's survival*

CEOs, and boards, should demand brief statements of brand health (equity) using the most sensitive measures from the section above to set beside their revenue statements. Without knowing if their brands are thriving or diseased, their accounts will be giving an incomplete picture. Most companies have their brand information spread around the organization; collecting it together into focussed brand equity statements will reveal its power. These statements should regularly appear in the board papers alongside the financials. Table 7.1 assumes that the top 10–20 metrics, which work for that particular company, have been selected, and they appear in column 2.

Measurement and assessment are just the beginning. Brands need the commitment of human, as well as financial, resources. Living beings need light, preferably sunshine, from above. The CEO needs to cherish the company's brands: take care of brand equity and that will take care of the shareholders.

**Table 7.1    Sample brand equity monitor**

| Relationship | Selected metrics | Latest actual | Change in year | Change vs. plan | 3 or 5-year trend |
|---|---|---|---|---|---|
| Consumer | Awareness Loyalty, innovation etc. | | | | |
| Trade customer | Distribution, sales etc. | | | | |
| Competitive | Market share etc. | | | | |

## Harmonizing metrics internationally

Table 7.1 applies to a brand's national market. While any marketer is interested in that brand's equity and how it is changing over time, it is highly unlikely that national marketers will provide themselves with metrics in anything like that format unless there has been some international and/or board level intervention.

National marketers will also be concerned with fire-fighting, diagnostics and short-term performance indicators, and with the behavior of the key players in their networks. Being at least once removed from the action lends some enchantment. Internationalists can observe, market by market, which measures work and, especially, which are sensitive and predictive.

One beginning is to collect each country's measures of PASSION and performance and test the similarities and differences. Our (informal) research around the world indicates that international marketers are less likely to be overwhelmed by measures than appalled by their absence. One reason is that brand equity measures need at least three years to be useful (to establish trends), which is well beyond the job expectancy of most national marketers. Lesser developed countries have little formal research available even if they had the resources to pay for it.

The next stage is to develop common language to the extent that measures can be understood and compared across national borders. Shared metrics emerge from theoretical and pragmatic challenge and debate, followed by modeling, in much the same way as at the national level above. But there is a difference. A single marketing unit should standardize its metrics, but a multinational needs to allow for some diversity. "Harmonization" is preferred to full standardization (unison) for a number of reasons. In choral terms harmony provides a richer experience, but without discords. The notes are related. If countries have different measures of volume (cases of 10 and 12 litres, for example), they need not be forced to standardize so long as the conversion ratio is widely understood. Metrics that work in one country may not do so in another, but that should be determined *empirically* and not on the basis of management prejudice.

Harmonization allows individual countries both to maintain the metrics that work best for them and also to experiment with new metrics. Discords can then be abandoned. A standard system would be rigid. At the same time, the ability to translate enables learning to cross borders. For this reason, get tough about harmonization. For example, consider appointing a single global market research agency. Other marketing service agencies, e.g. advertising, do not need to be global, but measurement is so critical to cross-border learning and cross-border learning is so much the *raison d'être* for international marketing that, today, we would have little hesitation in employing a single global market research agency for the main brand tracking studies. Obviously *ad hoc* and focus group work are different. Let the professional researchers sort out the nuances of cross-border translation so that all marketers, national and international, can get the learning.

The process of harmonizing metrics internationally is itself SILK: the implicit exchanges are more important than the explicit. In other words, the process of sharing these concepts may be even more important learning than the formal measurement system that ultimately emerges. Some firms need external assistance from consultants or advertising agencies to bring this about; some manage it by themselves. The *process* for establishing brand essence and brand equity measures should be integrated. Thus, standardize process, but harmonize metrics.

We have provided examples of marketing performance metrics, but not a definitive list, partly because they are context dependent and partly because this process of establishing the relevant measures is so important. It is better to learn how to fish than to be given fish, assuming, of course, that one has access to the fishing grounds. Access is determined by relationships, and money. SILK places some obligation on an international firm's HQ to underwrite cross-border learning costs, i.e. market research. Thus the role of the international marketer is to ensure that each local company measures PASSION and marketing performance to understand what they do, and why. Successful international marketers learn before they teach. Issues include:

- What measures are used, explicitly or implicitly, to measure PASSION, short-term performance and brand equity.

- Which customer segments are considered.

- How the measures are calculated. Much confusion results from using the same word, e.g. "loyalty," to mean different things.

- How often the measures are collected (once a year is OK, twice is better, more than that may well be redundant – depending on the nature of the business).

- Who, in the local company, sees these figures (just the brand manager, the marketing department or all senior management?).

- How they influence what the company actually does.

Confidentiality may be problematic. Brand equity measures are arguably the most important and, therefore, the most sensitive data the company possesses. Good relationships would be helped by the information flow being two-way: the nationals supply their data in exchange for seeing the whole picture. At the same time, the global brand manager may be reluctant to provide this information to a junior local manager who may job-hop to the competition the following week. Then there are distributors and other external partners. On the other hand, learning is clearly facilitated by the data warehouse being truly communal.

Sophisticated companies design their systems with the accent on self, rather than third-party control, and on openness. The Math component of future planning compares metrics against past performance as an intrinsic element of today's learning. Transnational comparisons introduce this learning to other business units and vice versa. Exposing the performance variances is more comfortable if the experience is shared. Thus control becomes part of planning, where it can be translated to performance.

Mid-year (month-to-month) controls are important as well. Retail businesses control themselves day-to-day as well as week-to-week. Planned actions constantly have to be refined in the light of performance, competition and the changing environment, but constant demands from international HQ to be kept informed of results and re-forecasts are, more often than not, excessive. Coaching is not the same as playing; international managers should ensure that control exists: they should not be the controllers.

The balance between empowerment and control determines the last practical aspect of international marketing metrics: presentation. If metrics are harmonized, they can be added up for the whole world and summarized on a single page. Others stop just a little short of that. Grand Metropolitan, now Diageo, believes that global numbers conceal more than they reveal. They harmonize the metric headings but present the measures column by column for the key countries with a single "all other" column. Since that leaves no room for comparative columns, trends are shown by the now common "traffic lights" system (green for improving, red for worsening and yellow for static) and symbols. They find that the color impressions are more valuable than the numbers themselves.

On the other hand, if metrics differ widely country by country, this columnar approach will not be feasible and international managers will need more ingenuity, e.g. using groups of metrics, as shown in Table 7.2. One way or another, the international marketer needs to find ways to present marketing performance metrics in a comparable fashion.

**Table 7.2    Some brand equity metrics**

| Category | Metric | Definition/comment |
|---|---|---|
| **Consumer/end user intermediate** | Awareness | Prompted, unprompted or total (both added together) |
| | Perceived quality/esteem | How highly rated |
| | Relevance to consumer | "My kind of brand" |
| | Salience | Prominence, stand-out |
| | (Perceived) differentiation | How distinct from other brands |
| | Commitment/purchase intent | For example, "will buy next time" |
| | Personality/identity | |
| | Attitudes | For example, liking |
| | Knowledge | Cognitive familiarity with attributes |
| **Consumer/end user behavior** | Total number of consumers | |
| | Period-to-period loyalty/retention | |
| | New consumer acquisitions | |
| | Price sensitivity/elasticity | Volume change of price changed |
| | Number/range of products per consumer/customer | Shows how many different products the typical consumer uses from the brand portfolio |
| | Number of leads generated/inquiries | |
| | Conversions | Proportion (by number) of leads who buy |
| | User demographics/ psychographics | |
| | Usage or purchase patterns | Seasonality |
| | Expressed complaints/dissatisfaction | |
| | Warranty expenses | Costs of correcting quality |
| **Trade customer/ retailer** | Sales | Value and/or volume |
| | % discount | |
| | Cost per contact | |
| | Distribution | Number of stores |
| | Share of shelf | |
| | Features in store | Number of times per annum |
| | Pipeline stockholding | Number of days inventory in the channel |
| | % sales on deal | Proportion of turnover "bought" |
| | Satisfaction/complaints | |

**Table 7.2    continued**

| Category | Metric | Definition/comment |
|---|---|---|
| **Relative to competitor** | Market share volume (SOM* Vol) | |
| | Relative price (SOM Val/SOM Vol) | |
| | Competitive response time | Days between competitive change in market and response |
| | Share loyalty | Share of category requirements |
| | Penetration | % of total who buy brand in period |
| | Relative end user satisfaction | Index of satisfaction as % of brand leader's satisfaction |
| | Relative perceived quality | Perceived quality as % of leader |
| | Share of voice | Advertising as % of total market |
| | Weight ratio (w.r.) | Indicator of whether customers are heavy (w.r. > 1) or light (w.r. < 1) users: w.r. = SOM/{penetration x share loyalty} |
| **Innovation** | Number of new products in period | Launches |
| | Satisfaction from new products | User data |
| | Perceived quality of new products | User data |
| | Revenue of last 3 years' products | % of total sales |
| | Margin of last 3 years' products | % of total gross margin |
| | Diffusion parameter | Speed of take-up by the market |
| | New season products/total products | |
| **Financial** | Gross margins | |
| | Gross margins of new customers | |
| | Cost of new customer acquisition | |
| | Marketing spend | |
| | Profit/Profitability | Contribution, trading, NPBT* NPAT |
| | Shareholder value/EVA/ROI* | |
| | Stock cover | Days of inventory |
| | Number of units on rent | |

*  SOM = Share of market    NPAT = Net profit after tax    NPBT = Net profit before tax
   EVA = Economic Value Added (a more sophisticated profit calculation)
   ROI = Return on Investment

# Executive notes

- Measurement is critical for performance (what you get), learning across borders, control and, most of all, symbolic declaration of what matters to management

- Measures of PASSION may be rudimentary but they will be none the worse for that. The international marketer should take care of PASSION and brand equity and let others take care of the profit and loss account

- Performance has two components: short-term results and the change in brand equity (the marketing asset) during the period

- A brand is a combination of product, packaging, identification, and image

- Brand equity is the owner's continuing intangible asset (or liability if things have gone horribly wrong) arising from marketing activities

- The brand exists mostly as memories in the minds of consumers/end users and the other market-place players

- Consumers are active participants in the creation of brand equity, which is based on the whole brand, not just identification and image. Measures of brand equity need to be consistent with the essence of the brand

- Brand equity can be measured in many ways of which valuation is just one

- An organization should begin with an excessive number of performance metrics and then allow those that are sensitive, predictive, reliable and economic to come to the fore

# References

1. Sheppard, A. (1994) "Adding Brand Value" in P. Stobart (ed) *Brand Power.* London: Macmillan, p. 98.
2. Berry, L. (1997) "Multiple Method Listening – the Building of a Service Quality Information System," Academy of Marketing Conference, Manchester.
3. For a comprehensive guide to brand equity see Keller, K. L. (1997) *Strategic Brand Management: Building, measuring and managing brand equity.* Upper Saddle River, NJ: Prentice Hall.
4. Rose, S. P. R. (1993) *The Making of Memory.* London: Bantam Books.
5. This section draws on the "Marketing Metrics" research project sponsored by the Marketing Council, Marketing Society, Institute of Practitioners in Advertising, and Sales Promotions Consultants Association (all UK) and Marketing Science Institute (USA). The conclusion will be published in 2000 by *FT Management.*
6. For examples of brand equity metrics, *see* Keller, K. L. (1997) *Strategic Brand Management: Building, measuring and managing brand equity.* Upper Saddle River, NJ: Prentice Hall; Aaker, D. A. (1991) *Managing Brand Equity.* New York: Free Press; Winters, L. C. (1991) "Brand Equity Measures: Some Recent Advances." *Marketing Research*, Vol. 3, December, pp. 70–73.
7. Based on Styles, C. and Ambler, T. (1997) "Brand Equity: Measuring what matters," *Australasian Journal of Market Research*, Vol. 5, No. 1, pp. 3–10.
8. For example, Dwyer, F. R. *et al.* (1987) "Developing Buyer–Seller Relationships," *Journal of Marketing*, Vol. 51, pp. 11–27 April.
9. Ford, D. *et al.* (1998) *Managing Business Relationships.* London: Wiley.

# chapter 8

# Not Invented Here

## Internationalizing innovation

'Why is it that a bicycle remains upright
when in motion, but if still, falls over?'

*Source:* D. Knight[1]

Pillsbury created the US market for refrigerated dough products. They are contained in cylindrical cans to provide "biscuits," "crescent rolls" (croissants), bread sticks, small rolls and other baked goods. Supermarkets place the cans horizontally on shelves, which assists readability and greater stockholding.

In the 1970s, Pillsbury entered the British market with these products, but unsuccessfully. In 1991, they tried again with identical US packaging. The British marketing team knew better and a number of changes were made. Most significantly, the British knew that cans had to stand vertically. Retailer customers and the UK advertising agency agreed. Research was convened to "prove" it.

"Pillsbury" is legible lengthways on the can. Vertical writing is hard (for a Westerner) to read and "Pillsbury" will not fit horizontally on an upright can. There were other problems. Shelf impact works lengthways and shelves can carry more product. Vertical cans created out-of-stock problems.

A year later, the UK switched to horizontal cans with an immediate improvement in business. No one could remember then what the objection was (nor who made it).

Business has to build a momentum of change in order to progress, otherwise, like the bicycle, it falls over. The development of brands, products, and their advertising, may stand at rest now and then. But that strategy is not usually viable for long in a changing environment. On the other hand, if a multinational allows each national business to develop its new and existing product and advertising portfolio in its own way, the bicycle is bound to wobble as it steers in several directions.

*Business has to build a momentum of change in order to progress, otherwise, like the bicycle, it falls over*

This chapter faces up to the single greatest obstacle and frustration for international marketers: Not Invented Here (NIH), the resistance by national units to ideas from abroad.

We are concerned with:

- Taking product innovation across borders.
- Speed to market. When to open new markets in series and when in parallel. When the world was bigger, the international manager could watch and wait for national success to be apparent before merchandising in other countries. Now the competitors are watching and they will not wait.
- Coping with cultural diversity. Some believe that certain products, e.g. food, are culturally rooted and therefore hard to transfer across borders, whereas other products, such as technology, are easier because they are culturally neutral. How true is this?
- Internationalising communication. Great advertising demands high levels of creativity and innovation, and is the most visible and expensive aspect of most marketing plans (once the product has been developed). Advertising is also fun to create and can therefore create unproductive turf wars between country managers and agencies alike ("Why just dub over the English sound-track when we can shoot our own film!"). But how do we create world-class advertising for the world?

New product development and advertising have been compared to childbirth: conception is fun, but delivery is tough. Managers at the national level seek involvement in conception, are ambivalent about carrying and delivery, and claim parenthood only when the product graduates successfully. Other people's babies are markedly less attractive than one's own. Selling the joys of surrogate motherhood is part of the international manager's daily round.

## Taking product innovation across borders

The world is full of good ideas. The problem is to recognize the few that can make a real difference to the bottom line. Over 20,000 new products appeared on US supermarket and drugstore shelves in 1994, about 15 times more than 1970.[2] Only about 10 percent of those were on sale two years later. Only about 1 percent of new fast food products succeed. The odds are not encouraging. Nevertheless, those with low development and launch costs can profitably adopt the Spartan baby approach: put them all on the shelves and see which survive.

*The world is full of good ideas*

The vast majority of innovations are incremental. For example, marketers develop what already exists by:

- Understanding *consumer* needs, subtracting what is already available and then filling that gap
- Asking existing *business* customers what they want
- Brand extension and creating new sub-brands
- Being R&D driven without, necessarily, consumer perceptions
- Introspection.

The international marketer may have the luxury of watching national new product launches before taking a closer look at those few that survive, but this option is becoming less attractive. For reasons of speed, quality, and ensuring international suitability, international marketers need to be in at the birth, if not the conception. Does the innovation fit the brand positioning? Has another country come up with a similar, perhaps better, innovation that should be tried first? If the national innovation works, has international development been built in, for example avoiding words like "mist" and "nova" that don't travel well? With questions like these, the international marketer stands a good chance of being cast as the wicked fairy at the christening.

By then it is too late. Social information about innovation needs to be imbedded into the culture: directly between national units and not just via the international manager when he drops by. Cross-border learning cannot be imposed; the best that top management can do is to create the climate where cross-border learning is desired and rewarded. Indeed, if they can do that, they do not need to do much else.

The international manager can adopt three strategies for cross-fertilizing innovation, using different strategies for different countries and/or innovations:

- *Passive.* Here he encourages national units to share innovations, and learn from each other, but takes no active role to push particular developments. In this "butterfly" approach, he cross-fertilizes the ideas, but adds nothing of his own.

- *Pacemaking.* Here he forms a portfolio of the best recent national innovations and uses incentives, e.g. funding research, to persuade other nationals to adopt or beat them. If the new country does, in fact, have a superior innovation then that replaces the old one in the portfolio. Coca Cola uses this approach for its advertising.

- *Participative.* In the previous strategies, the international manager had no "ownership" of the innovations and could therefore present himself as an objective, non-partisan representative of the shareholders. This has political advantages, but relies on national units providing world class products. If the global market demands a global product, e.g. automobiles, national innovation is not enough. International task forces may be formed or global development centers become responsible for the innovation. Allowing the national units to go into competition with these international developments may be healthy, but is more likely to result in waste, lack of co-operation, and friction. In this "worker bee" approach, the international manager not only cross-fertilizes, but does more. He has an active role in determining the more profitable areas and building resources for the future.

Upstream-weighted costs perhaps favor central development, downstream favor local development. In other words, highly technological products are more suitable for global marketing, service products for local. Exceptions to this rule – McDonald's, for example – does not detract from the use of the value chain in this analysis. Note "value chain" rather than "supply chain": the key is to identify what end users most value.

The choice of strategy depends on the market and the development costs. The cost of developing new pharmaceuticals, for example, drives global scale; hence the 1990s witnessed a wave of pharmaceutical mergers. To a lesser extent the choice of strategy depends on national cultures. When Mary Kay introduced its cosmetics brand to China, its basic marketing strategy had to be modified. In the USA, local saleswomen entertained potential clients at home. The Chinese saleswomen did not have large enough apartments and, in any case, such hospitality would have been seen as inappropriate. The strategy here was participative.

We regard Social Information as the key. Unless a sense of global identity can be achieved, NIH will prevail. There is a simple rule of thumb. The stronger the corporate culture within national units, i.e. shared beliefs, the greater the barriers to change.[3] For culture we like MIT Professor Ed Schein's definition: "The way in which a group of people solve problems."[4] Successful national innovation therefore militates against the acceptance of international innovation.

Also, the larger and more successful the business unit and its host market, the less it welcomes experience from outside – the USA, Germany, Japan and the UK provide good examples. Success reinforces the beliefs that led to that success (MAC) and rejects outside information inconsistent with those beliefs. Yet marketing is inherently cyclical. Yesterday's success provides the seeds of tomorrow's failure: nemesis follows hubris, thus failure → learning → success → failure. International managers have to remove boundaries around country units and replace them with a single boundary around the global firm. In sharing ways to solve problems (SILK), they need to build the desire to learn and then the learning from both success and failure.

One (albeit expensive) approach to the pro-active option is to create multinational teams. Jane Salk compared three product development teams and concluded that these factors determined success:[5]

- Teams that confronted early threats to their performance set aside internal differences.
- Equality in national representation, power and influence was divisive, i.e. the UN approach does not work.
- Their general managers, outside and senior to the joint venture, played a critical role fostering either integration and co-operation within the group, or hostility.

The same brand products should not necessarily be standardized around the world. Nescafé, for example, has many formulations around the world, as do the leading cigarette brands. The key issue is whether these are responses to real and significant consumer taste differences, or whether they are simply managerial perceptions. Standardization versus adaptation issues are rarely subject to rational resolution through market research. The same data, used selectively, will make a case for either.

Sterling Health grew from an aspirin business originally started by Bayer, which invented the product in Germany in the nineteenth century. Sterling acquired full US rights to Bayer Aspirin as part of World War I reparations, but the situation in the rest of the world was less clear and lengthy litigation ensued.

By the late sixties, Bayer had reacquired its UK aspirin business but Sterling also had a strong business in the UK. When a new, and arguably better, analgesic became available, Sterling UK was quick to launch it as Panadol, which became brand leader and is still in the top rank 20 years later. The US operation was fat and happy with its version of Bayer Aspirin, brand leader at that time. So the field was left to a small firm marketing acetaminophen (paracetamol).

They called it Tylenol, made a lot of money and sold out to Johnson & Johnson, who made a lot more. Tylenol now dominates the US analgesic market. Ten years too late, Sterling introduced Panadol to the USA claiming that it had not previously been possible to offer US consumers this important overseas pain killer.

*Source:* Mann, C. C. and Plummer, M. L. (1991) The Aspirin Wars. New York: Knopf, A.

## Speed to market

The option of waiting for national success before rolling out internationally is becoming less viable for three reasons. First, competitors can observe your national success and "me-one" you in other markets.[6] Second, any product with global ambitions needs to be tested in a variety of markets. Once tested successfully, it may as well be launched. Third, pressure from top management for quick results does not allow a waiting period.

The need for speed is increased by perceptions of shortening product life cycles, reduced consumer loyalty, and rapid boredom with what was once new. In this scenario, if you do not catch the moment, it is gone. Furthermore your competitor, aided by EPOS (electronic point of sale) data capture, is watching your every move. Therefore, speed to launch, while important, is not sufficient; one has to consider the entire cycle through to market penetration and back to the replacement of that newly won share by the next product in R&D.

Professor Tom Robertson of the Goizueta Business School has five recommendations for reducing market penetration time:[7]

- Reach the market first, i.e. start as soon as you can, not when the testing is complete.
- Pre-announce the new product. By saying your (superior) product is coming customers may be inhibited in stocking up with a rival brand.
- Innovate constantly.
- Occupy the market, e.g. fill up the shelves and pipelines.
- Track penetration, i.e. dynamic information systems following individual purchases and repurchases.

Speed to market requires simpler, faster decision processes, especially for international decisions. The Nestlé organization of the 1980s had complex central structures trying to make supra-national decisions, leading to conflict with national operations. Autonomy for local decision makers brought NIH in its trail.

Although top marketers scorn it, "me-too" marketing happens everywhere, especially in the US. If the first mover in a new sector can achieve acceptance and early domination of distribution (two big ifs), then, by and large, the first mover retains both the largest market share and premium price (in premium markets). Thus, successful first movers may suffer the risks and costs of starting up but will have a wonderful profit flow thereafter.

If the early results from the pioneer are attractive, a flood of me-too brands appears, offering the same product or one with minor advantages.

Their strategy is to exploit the bridgehead and/or destroy the first mover's advantage (and perhaps destroy the category). Their main advantage is, typically, price.

"First mover advantage" has been the subject of some debate.[8] Today's brand leaders appear to have been the innovators, but that can be explained by the demise of the original pioneers. Pioneers are likely to be ambushed by those already in the market. The moral is to expect the ambush. A new, poorly resourced company has few options. Teaming up with an established business may work if they can be trusted. More often they will exhibit NIH. Another option, but high risk, is to let another firm pioneer and be ready to ride in on that with something better (not cheaper). Most probably pioneering is the only choice and the plan should involve either taking such high ground (e.g. high price) as to be out of range, or having powerful allies ready to roll. Establishing your product as the industry standard, particularly in technology markets, is important – more so than having the better mousetrap (look what happened, or rather didn't happen, to Beta videos and Apple software).

To prevent me-one launches, an international marketer has to move fast. Ed Artzt, then CEO of Procter & Gamble (P&G), referred to the global launch of their 2-in-1 (shampoo and conditioner) as a "discontinuity." Unilever, weakened by NIH problems, took 15 years (1975–90) to roll its Timotei brand shampoo out to 31 markets. P&G took just 4 years to cover 31 markets (1986–90). Today, P&G would consider that slow and would aim for more than one new country per month.

Speed requires global roll-outs to be in parallel – as synchronous as possible. That means that all major country brand managers have to share in the research and experience, however vicariously, of the early countries. It worked for Gillette (see the case study opposite).

## Coping with cultural diversity

While we do not intend to delve deeply into this complex topic, international managers clearly must be sensitive to cultural differences.

Professor Jean-Claude Usunier considers cultural aspects of product standardization and adaption.[9] His framework distinguishes:

- The physical attributes (size, weight, colour etc.). Asian cultures will advise that some colours, for example, are unlucky or associated with

Between 1986–8 Gillette fought off four takeover bids. The brand that had dominated shaving for so long was gradually losing its shine. Consumers couldn't tell the difference between one disposable and the next. Discounting became the norm. It wasn't much fun defending a 65 percent market share when margins were eroding.

To keep shareholders on side, the then chairman, Colman Mockler, promised a revolutionary shaving technology that would guarantee profits for years to come. Consumers would be able to tell the difference between this shaving system and competitors' and, more importantly, would be prepared to pay for it. This was the Gillette Sensor.

There were, essentially, two options for the Sensor launch in 1990. The first was the more cautious market-by-market method, where consumer reactions could be monitored and adjustments made along the way. The second was the simultaneous "North Atlantic" launch, which would cover the whole of North America and Europe in one hit. While potentially more risky, this would allow the launch to achieve critical mass, make a lot of noise, and achieve significant marketing efficiencies, e.g. the same advertising campaign could be used in each country. It also had the advantage of speed.

The second strategy was used and it worked. The advertising and publicity blitz generated substantial awareness and trial, and the conversion rate was excellent – 80 percent of men who tried Sensor kept on using it. By the end of 1990, Sensor blades and razors accounted for $200 million of Gillette's $1.6 million in shaving sales. The new product line was nearly profitable by the end of the first year. The only problem seemed to be keeping up with demand. By 1997, the Gillette Sensor family of shaving products outsold all competitive blade and razor products combined.

*Source:* based on "The best a plan can get," *The Economist*, 15 August 1992, pp. 61–62; reports in *The New York Times*, April/May 1998; www.gillette.com

death. Take such warnings seriously, but with a pinch of salt. Visits to markets will show up brand leaders that flout the rules.

- Service attributes. Some cultures prefer to serve themselves; others find it demeaning.
- Symbolic brand associations. Perhaps the most important, they are also the most subtle.

Smart global marketers do not de-nationalize their products. Levi's and McDonald's have done well internationally *because* they epitomize America to non-Americans. British Airways succeeds because it symbolizes the best of Britain, a fact the company seemed to have forgotten in 1997 when it repainted the tail fins with all those confusing artworks. Good marketers make their national characteristics attractive to other nationalities. Smirnoff does not come from Russia (except Black Label), nor Bacardi from Cuba, yet their brand leadership depends on their Russian and Caribbean heritage.

Cadbury had an immense success with its Wispa chocolate bar launched in the UK in 1982. The company's other launches of the period – Amazing Raisin, Aztec, Rumba, and Welcome – fell away, but Wispa found an immediate place in the consumer's repertoire. It combined the taste of Cadbury's Dairy Milk (CDM) with aeration, which increased mouth feel, perceived size and taste whilst reducing cost. CDM was launched by Cadbury in 1905 and was then, and still is, the brand leader. The Cadbury taste dominates the UK market with 30 percent of all chocolate and 50 percent of formed bars.[10]

UK success encouraged them to go for the USA. A £17 million plant was built on the East coast but the US launch failed.

Was market research inadequate? Not in our book: great new products regularly fail research for reasons seen in the Memory Affect Cognition (MAC) model of comprehension and decision making. The error was in failing to understand why Wispa did so well in the UK: an established (M) taste was being presented in a new way. The Cadbury taste had always done poorly in the USA, despite many attempts. Hershey has long dominated the moulded bar market. If they had launched Wispa with a Hershey taste, it may well have succeeded.

In coping with cultural diversity, we do not belittle the contribution that research and rational analysis, e.g. the Wispa bar, can make. Focus group and other qualitative research can be especially helpful. At the same time, cultural sensitivity ultimately comes back to empathy. Get into the foreign market and *feel* the para-social relationships between your brands and products and the consumers of that country. In so doing, sophisticated international marketers watch out for two types of people:

- Consumers who do not wait for marketers to cross borders. If they like products enough, they themselves import the innovations.
- High-performing market innovators.

Bailey's Irish Cream first entered the US market in the luggage of airline crews. Having sampled the product elsewhere, they brought it with them. In a shrinking world, product diffusion is increasingly both consumer and industrial customer driven.[11] Having the market opened up by consumers is not only encouraging for the brand's management but it also provides a powerful public relations advantage. Advertising may not be required.

Larry Huston, P&G's director of innovation and knowledge, benchmarked 180 high-performance innovators (managers) in 40 companies and found that they:[12]

- Are high "bandwidth" people: they know a lot about many different areas.
- Know the literature, the cutting edge and they build ways to keep in touch.
- Are knowledge driven, not technique and tricks driven. They believe that creativity without knowledge is fantasy.
- Ask the right questions. How to get the right questions is the issue.
- Select a breakthrough goal that drives the above.
- Operate on many hypotheses all the time. They know that problems can be solved in many ways and they develop multiple, competitive, robust hypotheses.

Huston, like Stefano Marzano at Philips, believes in asking naive, childlike questions. Not every international marketer personally needs these high innovation characteristics, but the network must contain at least one.

People of all kinds take ideas across borders, not just international marketers. The momentum may be far stronger when they have been adopted by consumers or national marketers. Tuning will be needed, but such is the difficulty of national borders; internationalists are pragmatic about any help they can get.

## International advertising

### Lufthansa to take long-term, local approach

Loof-thanz-sa … Rhoof-tahn-zuh … Luft-anz-ah. The name "Lufthansa" just doesn't seem to roll off the tongue for many Koreans.

What's more, given the airline's previous corporate advertising campaign, which made virtually no sense to locals – even with correct translations, the name Lufthansa hasn't become any easier to pronounce. As one of the world's major airlines, which is known for its service, Lufthansa plans to run a completely new advertising campaign in 1999, one which specifically targets a local audience.

With the services of its advertising agency, Dentsu, Young and Rubicam Korea, Lufthansa plans to spend about one-half of its 1998 ad budget on locally-created ads, which will first appear in the print and outdoor media some time in March or April.

"We acknowledge that the corporate advertising campaign for Lufthansa world-wide was not effective here," says Lufthansa Korea general manager, Werner D. Graessle. "The advertising message for Korea could be quite different than it is in another country," he continued.

Graessle will now concentrate on building brand awareness for the airline.

One example of how committed Lufthansa Korea is to localizing its operations is its decision to postpone the launch date of a world-wide corporate advertising campaign surrounding the new first- and business-class concept.

"If we advertise this new corporate campaign next month, we run the risk of confusing our customers here in Korea," says Graessle. "While promoting this concept beforehand may have its advantages, we can't afford to lead our customers on. Especially since we're here for the long-term."

Source: *Korea Herald*, 14 January 1998

Positive experiences with your product (M) help create satisfaction, trust, and, hopefully, commitment (A) in the brand–consumer relationship. Buying decisions should then, more often than not, go your brand's way (C). Communication can work in a similar manner. But communication across borders and cultures is challenging, to say the least. International marketers face a number of dilemmas.

One of the authors was asked to advertise female sanitary products in a conservative and religiously divided Lebanon using straight talking and visually blatant US/European copy formats, which had been decreed as global ads. With relatively small revenue prospects, and resources, the simple choice was whether to run them or not.  In the event, they were adapted only slightly and, though controversial, they were extremely successful, particularly in very quickly generating widespread awareness. Of course, international advertising does not necessarily mean a single campaign. Some, such as Shell in 1997/8 and British Airways go that way, but most, like Lufthansa, prefer to tailor their ads, to some extent, to the local community.

A theme of this book is the international organization as a single organism, which learns primarily from experience and secondly from implicit information and shared feelings. Only occasionally do firms learn from the objective, quantitative data that make up the traditional mechanical model of the firm. Analytic learning is important and we force ourselves to do it, but it is not easy. Our new perspective highlights the importance of sharing social information between the members of the firm and its close associates (suppliers and distributors, for example) and of the linkage between decision making and affect.

When advertising is central to building brand equity, as it so often is, the marketers are right to involve their ad agencies deeply and not regard them as just another set of suppliers. However, treating the agency as part of the client organization poses a number of problems because:

- The agency has different goals.
- The number of potential connections in a network grows geometrically with the number of participants.
- A multinational client, working with a multinational agency, multiplies borders and politics.
- When both agency and client are not truly global firms, the agency structure is unlikely to match that of the client. The client may use a miscellany

of agencies around the world and may itself have a mixture of subsidiary and third-party national operations with varying degrees of control.

There used to be a strong case for international marketers to avoid all advertising agency contacts. Client–agency relationships were confined to the national level. But the trend to globalization and the need for cross-border learning have removed this option for the largest companies.

To save duplication, maximize cross-border learning and reduce total production costs, the Pronto (an international soft drink) account was placed with Ad-Global, a world-wide agency formed by the Sirial twins when they broke away five years ago. Pronto has now been with Ad-Global (known to its competitors as Subtract-Local) for 12 months. Pronto's national brand managers have brought these items to the attention of their global HQ:

- Producing transnational advertising is demotivating the local teams. The transnational ads, in trying not to offend anyone, are boring and banal
- Apart from the possibility that they will lose their existing business to another agency(ies), there is no financial incentive to save costs; 17.65 percent of production costs form a significant part of agency income. Local agencies are insisting on local production in order to tailor the transnational work to cultural nuances
- The nature of the relationship between a key international marketer and the agency's global client service director is causing speculation. Do they need to travel so much together?
- International co-ordination has added to costs, meetings and paperwork. Benefits are not clear
- The global appointment had been strongly influenced by the high ad-production costs market by market. Despite centralised production, costs had not decreased. For example, one pan-European commercial was shot on one location to save costs. For local tailoring and language, all national teams were present, bringing one or two of their own actors and directing a few scenes to reflect local preferences. It was essentially a single one-minute commercial, with local variation. The final cost was greater than the sum of the previous separate ones.

Introducing the international dimension can confuse. Even so, there is merit in the long tradition of using ad agencies as outsourced marketing help. Agency staff turnover is generally slower than that of their multinational clients, especially at the national level, and the agency may genuinely have better and longer brand experience and understanding. For over 100 years, agencies have represented themselves as the spokespeople of the consumer. Agencies push for more spending on brand equities than do managers with an eye on quarterly earnings.

Global ad campaigns do not need global agencies. Bartle, Bogle and Hegarty (BBH) masterminded the international campaign for Levi's from a single office in London, though they have since opened an office in New York. Other one-stop shops have argued that their product is easier to take across borders precisely because they do not have the complexity of inter-office politics. Colgate-Palmolive long struggled to get the Paris and London offices of Young & Rubicam to agree on campaigns.

Long years of watching these debates have led us to the conclusion that decisions to globalize or localize advertising and ad agencies have little to do with the market-place and everything to do with internal factors. International marketers are usually biased toward international campaigns. Given enough strength of personality and corporate support, they win. But some opt, such as Coca Cola and McDonald's, for diversity. Attempting to globalize in an organization dominated by national barons will fail as surely as a democratic approach in a culture yearning for central direction.

*Global ad campaigns do not need global agencies*

We could stop considering at this point whether global advertising is appropriate: if you *know* what is right, further commentary will not change your mind. If you do not know what is right, globalizing is not for you. Nevertheless, it may be helpful to apply some key lessons to international advertising from previous chapters:

- Divide the company's brand portfolio into three groups: potentially global, those where some cross-border learning will help performance, and strictly local.

- Ignore the last group and set some "pacemaker" (best practice) processes up to cross-fertilize, using social information, the international group. The rest of these points concern the first, potentially global, group only.

- Decide, by whatever means, whether to have a global agency, independent national agencies with one office serving as global co-ordinator, or independent agencies with you as the international marketer, acting as co-ordinator.

- Determine the priority of the brands in terms of attention. In a large firm, different international marketers may each be working on a different brand, possibly in co-ordination and possibly using the same agency(ies). In a one-year period, it is unlikely any single international marketer can do this job for more than one brand.

- Determine the global brand positioning and essence using the (new?) agency network (*see* Chapter 5). Then, using the key elements of the positioning, establish the framework for local variation.

- Determine the extent of global and local. This is not either/or; the international marketer is seeking both global learning and local relevance. The difference is whether it proceeds top down or bottom up. In the top-down case the global marketer approves the world-wide campaign, subject to agreed rules for localization. In the bottom-up case, only the positioning and essence, with local variations, are centrally approved, leaving locals free to work within them. The international marketers then seek convergence through cross-fertilizing the best local campaigns.

- Harmonize brand equity measurement world-wide so that campaign briefings and assessments use the same metrics.

There is no one-fits-all solution to international advertising. On the other hand, there are some sure routes to failure:

- Designing global ads without considering processes and relationships
- Trying to do too much with too little power and resources
- Fudging positioning
- Allowing national borders to keep learning out
- Indulging agencies: providing tight briefs based around quantified objectives and brand equity metrics stimulates, rather than diminishes, great creativity
- Dependence on market research and, worse, allowing it to be used for political purposes.

In the future, global ad agencies are likely to play an increasingly important role as surrogate international marketing managers. We have noted two logistical problems for these managers, the high resource and traveling costs for their local hosts, and the need for international marketing managers to be everywhere during the planning season – two months of the year perhaps, and nowhere for the rest of the time. Coupled with this are two trends that will not go away: globalization, which makes such visits more necessary, and cost cutting, which makes them less possible.

Video conferencing will help, of course. But using a global advertising agency's network to build and measure brand equity, to keep a focus on brand positioning, can be valuable. Coins have two sides and this route might open the door, as mentioned above, to negative factors. It does, however, have the great advantage of putting considerable extra resources into play during the planning season and not carrying those costs at other times. International marketers should think hard about how to carry SILK across those extra organizational borders in order to reap greater benefits at less cost.

When all is said, however, only for some companies is advertising the key driver of brand equity. Moët et Chandon champagne grew to be brand leader without advertising at all.

## Using other media such as fairs and PR

The same loonies who think brands are dead tell us that mass media advertising is finished. The new networked age is one-to-one, they say. They are wrong: technology provides new media, but the old do not die. At most, they fade away.

Our ancestors developed the power of speech because one-to-one physical grooming took too long.[13] Physical grooming is still more fun but nowadays one has to be careful in one's choice of groomees. Caxton and others gave us the printed word. Britain's King George V was able to talk to the then British Empire through the miracle of wireless telegraphy before muttering "bugger Bognor" and expiring.[14] New media are constantly being discovered, the marketer's choice increases and thereby becomes more confusing. Media influence the messages that can be carried and the likely responses to those messages. Media determine who will receive the messages, and how. Conversely, the required responses and the target market influence the type of media needed.

Thus (mass) advertising will continue to meet the needs of (mass) consumer packaged brand marketers. As the target shrinks in size and messages become more sophisticated, other media become increasingly attractive. Advertising is less significant to business-to-business marketers. Pheasant shooting, at $5,000 per person per day, may be a cost-efficient medium. Non-verbal messages might still be carried best by physical groomers. So far as we know, this service is not available for brand marketers, but we would not be surprised. The wheel would have turned full cycle, but also moved on.

## Intel and Yahoo!

Intel, the world's leading computer chip maker, and Yahoo!, a start-up that has become the leading internet media group, stumbled into the business of building global brands almost by accident.

For Intel, the lights went on in 1989. An advertising campaign, aimed at urging computer manufacturers to switch to its latest microprocessor, the 386, had the surprising side-effect of persuading consumers to ask for 386-based computers. At the time, says Dennis Carter, Intel vice-president and director of marketing, "I didn't really know what a brand was. But it became evident that we had created a brand and that it made a difference in consumers' purchase plans."

The next step was to brand not merely one product but the whole range, using the now-familiar "Intel inside" logo. Intel launched the campaign in 1991 with its first "co-operative advertising" programme, offering to share the costs of advertising with computer manufacturers that used Intel chips. Soon after came the first "Intel inside" TV commercial – a journey through the innards of a personal computer, ending up at the microprocessor stamped with Intel's logo.

It had become the first semiconductor company to hawk its product to consumers as though it were a new cola. Intel initially tailored its advertising to different markets. In Japan, for example, the logo read "Intel in it," but was abandoned when the company found the "Intel inside" brand was better recognized because of information from the US.

"This really drove home the homogeneity of the global PC market," said Carter. Since then, its logo has appeared in more than $3.4 billion (£2.1 billion) worth of advertising – including spending by PC manufacturers – according to Intel.

In comparison, Yahoo!'s marketing resources are meagre. But the web navigation service has made full use of the global reach of the internet to build its name, relying heavily on users to spread the word. Yahoo! grew out of a list of favourite websites maintained by two Stanford University students. Although theirs was one of hundreds of similar hobbyist web guides at the time, it drew followers with its contemporary style and catchy name.

"A big portion of what has put Yahoo! on the map is just great word of mouth," says Karen Edwards, director of brand management. In particular, Yahoo! built a grassroots following among the many newcomers to the internet, who regarded the service as a friendly "home base" among the confusion of the web. Yahoo! also attracted users at minimal cost through strategically placed "hyperlinks" on other websites, such as the home page of Netscape Communications, the leading supplier of web-browser software.

The start-up company demonstrated the potential of the internet for building global brands, a lesson that has not been lost on bigger companies. Even before Yahoo! spent money on traditional advertising, it was attracting users worldwide. Last year it began advertising on television and radio in an attempt to encourage "near surfers" – people not yet online but who are interested in taking the plunge – to use its services.

"When we went out and advertised on television early last year, it was every last penny we had," Ms Edwards recalls. But the move paid off by helping Yahoo! to differentiate itself from a growing band of competitors achieving broader brand recognition. Last spring, the group launched its initial public offering, providing extra funds for more advertising and expansion of its services. Yahoo! is the most highly valued internet media company, with a market capitalisation of $2.3 billion. An estimated average of 5 million computer users go to Yahoo!'s web pages every day.

About 30 percent of visitors to Yahoo!'s website are from outside the US and the company has also established web guides aimed at international markets.

Even as Yahoo! is making more use of "old media" to promote its brand name, Intel is moving on to the web. The semiconductor company is among the biggest spenders on the "banner ads" that adorn many web pages.

*Source:* Kehoe, L. and Denton, N.
*The Financial Times* 23 October 1997

Other marketing communication media include:

- Public relations, in the sense of planned acquisition of editorial column inches or the broadcast equivalent. José Cuervo Tequila rose to leadership in the USA on beach volleyball sponsorship and coverage. Their advertising was extensive, but was not highly rated.

- Direct marketing through mail or telephone or, now, the internet.

- Network marketing, pioneered by Tupperware and since adopted by Mary Kay and Amway. The aim of the sale is to acquire new representatives as well as sell product. This should be distinguished from personal home selling, e.g. Avon, though the divide is thin.

- Shows, e.g. trade, industrial and agricultural events. Again close to selling, but the role of the show, especially for industrial products, may be to build relationships (brand equity) with sales at a later date.

- Trade media. As they are read more by competitors than customers, one should be careful of trade vehicles for building relationships. Even so, their role can be valuable.

We believe that the same basic rules, rehearsed for international advertising above, can be applied to other consumer and trade media.

Assessment, however, is even more difficult as the effects of the different media and marketing mix elements are well nigh impossible to separate. This leads some, probably rightly, to plan and evaluate marketing campaigns as holistically as they can. Advertising and promotions go together. Integrated marketing communications (IMC) bring all media into a single co-ordinated package.[15]

## Executive notes

- This chapter addresses the business of moving innovation across borders. The first and greatest of the 4Ps is the product itself. Whatever the appeal of price, promotion and distribution, end-user satisfaction is ultimately determined by the product

- Marketers recognize the importance of innovation at the national level. Accepting innovation from abroad is another matter. Just as innovation is the lifeblood of marketing, "Not Invented Here" is the leukemia. NIH saps the ability of business units to learn across borders and gain the benefits of world experience

- Corporate learning does not happen by itself. The international marketer must build the climate in which national units are keen both to import and export lessons from experience. The desire to learn creates a readiness to review the knowledge cluttering the attic and discard what is no longer useful. Unlearning, however difficult, is needed to make space for learning that will create new value. Growth then requires the slow development of social information into implicit, and then explicit, learning and knowledge

- The international marketer, who is too creative, may create new walls. He must develop the process for maintaining existing product and packaging standards, finding improvements, and rolling them out around the world. Priority developments can be left either to the national marketers or global R&D centers, but not both. Secondary developments can be left to the nationals. The local or global preference should depend on the product sector: the higher the unit cost of developing prototypes, the more central they need to be. In any case, the marketer should be more concerned with removing borders than with "owning" the development

- A bicycle does not fall over, nor does a business, when it is covering new ground at a rapid pace. The faster it is going, the more stable, but also the more dangerous it is to attempt a rapid change of direction. International product development, likewise, needs momentum and consistent direction

- The decision to use global advertising is largely a matter of the personal commitment and skills of the international marketer, and the firm's culture. That does not dictate the parallel agency structure. Global agencies can create local campaigns and a one-shop agency can create a global campaign. Whether the firm drives advertising decision making top down or bottom up, the same WEM planning processes and brand equity metrics should be employed

- Thus other media, such as trade fairs and public relations, should be considered as part of integrated marketing communications, not as optional extras. Similarly, the relative importance of shifting brand equity in the minds of immediate customers versus end users should determine the priority of resources for trade and consumer communications

- But it all comes down to the destruction of borders to allow global learning. The Memory Affect Cognition model prevails. Do not even attempt to address this issue with words, logic and sweet reason until the M and A components are in place

# References

1. Knight, D. (1991) Unpublished article. London.
2. *New Product News* quoted in "How to Turn Junk Mail into a Goldmine – or Perhaps Not," *The Economist*, 1 April 1995, p. 81.
3. Lorsch, J. (1986) "Managing Culture: The invisible barrier to strategic change" *California Management Review* 28 (2 Winter) pp. 95–109. This is consistent with the Festinger research discussed in Chapter 2.
4. Schein, E. (1985) *Organizational Culture and Leadership.* San Francisco: Jossey-Bass.
5. Salk, J. E. (1993) "Behind the State of the Union: The design and social processes on relationships in shared management joint venture teams," MSI Report Number 93–110, July.
6. A "me-too" is the launch of a similar product in the same market. A "me-one" pre-empts the innovator by launching the similar product in a different country.
7. Robertson, T. (1993) "How to Reduce Market Penetration Cycle Times," *Sloan Management Review*, Fall, pp. 87–96.

8. Schnaars, S. P. (1994) *Managing Imitation Strategies*. New York: The Free Press.
9. Usunier, J. C. (1996) *Marketing Across Cultures*. 2nd edn. Upper Saddle River, NJ: Prentice Hall, Ch. 8.
10. Palmer, A. (1997) "Cadbury Ltd: Harnessing the strengths of the corporate brand," in Gilmore, F. (ed) *Brand Warriors*. London: Harper Collins, pp. 145–60.
11. Ganesh, J. and Kumar, V. (1996) "Capturing the Cross-National Learning Effect: An analysis of an industrial technology diffusion," *Journal of the Academy of Marketing Science*, 24 (4 Fall), 328–37.
12. Internet (Melnet) communication via Chris Macrae, 28 May 1997.
13. Mithen, S. (1996). *The Prehistory of the Mind*. London: Thames and Hudson. Dunbar, R. I. M. (1993) "Coevolution of Neocortical Size, Group Size and Language in Humans," *Behavioral and Brain Sciences* 16, pp. 681–735.
14. A British seaside resort, suggested to him as a place to recover.
15. Schultz, D. and Walters, S. J. (1998) *Measuring Brand Communication ROI*. Chicago: Association of National Advertisers.

# "Does this apply to me?"

## Adjusting for sectors

'It all depends on how we look at things, and not
on how they are in themselves'

*Source:* C. G. Yung[1]

---

TNT, an Australian logistics distribution company, wanted its salesforce to present a consistent and unified brand across 220 countries. The medium needed to be flexible to localise and accommodate a wide range of delivery systems.

Using a CD-ROM, each sales manager has full control over text, font and choice of 75 visuals from a library. They can import their own images.

"The crucial factor was being able to create a presentation tool that conveyed the global message in a consistent and integrated way, yet was flexible enough to take into account the regional variations," said Bob Johnson, TNT Worldwide's vice-president of sales and marketing.

*Source: Marketing*, London, p. 28, 21 August 1997

---

Just as managers perceive their countries and their customers as unique, so Not Invented Here plays across different sector boundaries. Here we discuss four sectors: business-to-business marketing, services, retailing, and the non-profit sector. Each provides challenges for the international marketing

*Relationships,
dialogue, and
connectivity are
central*

manager to create common purpose, manage SILK learning, and motivate positive animal spirits. Again, relationships, dialogue, and connectivity are central.

Relational concepts in marketing emerged from the industrial, business-to-business (b2b) and service sectors.[2] Whereas consumer (product) marketers were preoccupied by the impersonal determination of the marketing mix for customers they rarely saw, b2b and service marketers were personally engaged with customers. Of course each product sector is different: a power station is a far cry from toothpaste. Capital purchases differ from routine disposable goods, but much of the difference arises from the scale of the purchase rather than the type of customer. A capital purchase by an individual, such as a car or a house, has parallels with a capital purchase by a business. The relational perspective unifies consumer, b2b, and services marketing by personalizing the brand and empathizing with the end user as a single individual. All products, great and small, have individual end users.

*All products, great and
small, have individual
end users*

Does this mean that a packaged-goods consumer marketer can transfer painlessly from one sector to another? The evidence is against it. As the need for professional marketing has grown, executives have transferred from consumer packaged goods to the b2b sector with dismal results. Why so? Their competence and marketing skills were not to blame. The *relative* importance of different elements of the marketing mix changes but not the mix itself. Cognitively they could handle that task. But their experience, habits of thought (M) and feelings for the market (A) did not transfer.

## Business-to-business marketing

Business marketing, no different from consumer marketing, demands clarity about the relationships between end user, customer, competitor, and the brand. The positioning statement is as vital in b2b as in any marketing. The "brand" is more likely to be the reputation of the firm as a whole rather than what is seen on the packaging of a product, but the principles are the same. We may need to remind ourselves of the key difference between pan-company marketing to satisfy customers and the narrow function of marketing departments, which exist largely to motivate and then administer advertising and promotional budgets. Most industrial marketers have minimal advertising and promotional budgets. On the other hand, trade fairs occupy the equivalent position in the mix: they are vital to forming and building relationships and promoting the products.

All marketing is comprised of dyadic relationships between brand, customer and consumer, with the competition in the center, creating its own relationships, *see* Figure 9.1. Of course, relationships with competitors also matter. One's competitor in one market may be a customer in another. In the consumer area, also, manufacturers may sell to the public directly.

Some commentators treat industrial marketing as a relatively new discipline, distinguished from consumer marketing by a separate core of knowledge. The idea that industrial marketing merely shifts the goods into the first stages of the value chain, whereas consumer marketing deals with end users, is misleading. The emphasis differs, but both deal

*One's competitor in one market may be a customer in another*

with immediate customers *and* end users. Railroad locomotive manufacturers sell to high-level decision makers (the immediate customers). But those who use the trains, the drivers, the maintenance staff, and even the passengers, have opinions that need to be considered.

Industrial marketers should worry as much as packaged goods companies do about end users. The industrial marketer should "look through" the customer's business to see what happens to their products all the way to the end user, i.e. where the products sold lose their separate identity. If GKN, a

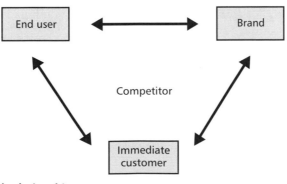

**Fig. 9.1    Brand relationships**

UK-headquartered, global industrial company, sells screws to an engineering firm, the end user of the engineered good neither knows nor cares whose screws were used. We must be wary of this distinction because some b2b marketers build their brand equity by advertising directly to consumers in order to help their b2b brand equity. "Intel inside" is one such example and branded sugar substitutes, such as Nutrasweet, are another. In the GKN case, the consumer was the operative who controlled the screw driving machine.

Everything about defining positioning and brand equity metrics thus far, remains equally valid. So too is the need to work back from the end user's point of view. A perfect b2b marketing proposition provides the end user with a better solution to his problem, allowing the marketer to charge a higher price, sell more and/or make them at a lower price. Churning out the same old screws rather faster and cheaper will not be successful in the long run.

We crystallize the differences between consumer and industrial in one word: complexity, though even this may be mostly in the eye of the beholder. For b2b marketing, more people may be involved, and customers are more likely to demand changes and innovation. For example, some industrial marketing is characterized by multiple buyers dealing with multiple sellers.

*Business marketing is fundamentally different from consumer marketing because of how organizations purchase products*

"Business marketing is fundamentally different from consumer marketing because of how organizations purchase products."[3]

We need to distinguish situations where the power or business size (not the same thing) is disproportionate from situations where both power, size and transactional importance are well balanced, i.e. the world of "middleweight purchasing," a term that describes the industrial buying situation between the heavyweight business of tender offers and the lightweight purchasing of consumables, which reflects normal consumer buying patterns.

General Motors' purchases of stationery are unimportant to them, but not to their stationery suppliers. Switching suppliers in the middleweight is administratively and emotionally expensive and inconvenient. The "Transaction Cost Analysis" field of economics seeks to address the reconciliation of free market transactional exchanges with the observed reality of continuous relational trading and vertical integration.[4] The costs of gathering information and using market processes undoubtedly play their part, but business continuity is not explained by economics alone.

A large part of big-ticket marketing, whether b2b or industrial, is risk reduction. In consumer capital goods, e.g. cars, the brand supplies much of the assurance, so it does in b2b with the reputation (brand) of the supplier. Small companies must find ways, especially for bespoke solutions, of supplying similar comfort levels. Even payment by results (when the machinery, say, is installed and working) may not be a solution because the lead time is part of the risk. Buyers cannot afford to fall behind or have some parts of the new line working and some not.

They solve the problem mostly by continuing to buy from those they know and who have proved reliable in the past. From the outside it looks like a trusting relationship. In fact we doubt that trust, in this sense, or transactional cost economics really exist as separate entities. The MAC model provides a simpler, more behavioral, explanation. Consider *guanxi*, which builds slowly between the Chinese on the basis of working together first in smaller things and then progressively in larger. In the same manner, buying habits between firms and their suppliers are first reinforced by experience, second by feelings, including the two social groups (supplier and buyer), and only finally does economic rationality fine tune the exchange.

Western business people fail to understand that Chinese buyers have usually decided who will supply *before* the invitations to tender go out. The purpose of the process is merely to use the market to fix the terms and conditions. Thus trust does not pre-exist and may only be a misreading of experiential development.

## International aspects of b2b marketing

We argue that b2b marketing differs in the relevant experience, memories, and personal contacts and empathy appropriate for each sector and country. Personal selling and trade fairs have more importance than advertising for immediate customers than end users, but these are all differences of emphasis. The MAC and SILK models apply equally. Marvin Baker's vicious cycle (see following case study) illustrates the dependency problem for some business marketers: if the inward products become key, will the customer trust some foreigner with whom he has not dealt previously?

"Despite the fact that the US market is among the largest and most open in the world, many European technology-based companies find it more difficult to penetrate than other export markets. In fact, at 50 percent, the success rate for European companies in the US is unnecessarily low."

Americans are actually quite conservative and do not believe the Europeans show enough commitment to offset the distance. They believe they will give priority to European customers. Yet these issues are rarely discussed. Instead we see a "vicious cycle," namely:

- Introduction of the European product. It is initially well-received so that the American can learn as much as possible about its performance. This is very encouraging to the European
- Undisclosed concern of the American about the European's commitment to the US market
- Refusal by the American to purchase the product until the European establishes his commitment
- Disappointment of the European
- Loss of money by the European in the US, eventually reaching his limit
- Withdrawal of the European from the US market
- Reconfirmation to the American that the European was not sufficiently committed to the US market, thus increasing his concern when the next European company approaches him

Source: Baker, M. L. (1993) "Breaking the Transatlantic Vicious Cycle," Venture Capital Review. London: European Venture Capital Association[5]

Relational variables, such as trust (but see above), commitment, loyalty, and relative power are more relevant measures than the traditional awareness and attitude measures of the neoclassical perspective. Building the habitual relationship needs different tools. Risk reduction is key. Some firms fly customers back to the exporting country at the *customer's* expense on the grounds that commitment breeds commitment. Others will send the machinery, withholding the invoice until the customer expresses satisfaction.

One upside is that the customer should become dependent on the new machine. One downside is that he could have it copied locally and then returned.

The higher the ticket, and the more dependency involved, the more carefully the relationship has to be developed. Almost certainly, the exporter has to establish at least one experienced staff member on the foreign soil who calls regularly. Nothing puts a proposal in the pending tray faster than the knowledge that the supplier has just caught the flight home. Habit formation requires regular contact.

National Finance (name changed for reasons of confidentiality), the leading US wholesale finance house in its sector, had become very frustrated by the London market, where they had established a branch three years earlier. Every major bid made it to the last three, but was then rejected. They had thought that roughly 33 percent would be accepted, as they knew all the offers were objectively comparable. The US used expatriates trained to understand the (complex) products and their advantages over European products. When the bids were rejected, the British teams were unfailingly polite, enquiring after their families back home. They were not expected to be staying.

The reputation of the firm can be expressed as brand equity metrics which can track the development of satisfaction. What those metrics will not do, here or in consumer marketing, is supply the creative thinking. Fortunately, some types of industrial customers supply most of the creative ideas themselves. MIT's Professor von Hippel found that more than 80 percent of innovation of scientific instruments came from the customers.[6] Accordingly, the b2b international marketer needs to develop superb listening skills.

Just as an international consumer marketer needs to get out to *see* the local market, before settling in for the SILK session with the local team, so the international b2b marketer needs to visit the key national customers to *listen* to what they want and to hear their views on future changes. The marketer needs to meet the end-user operatives and hear the problems they are trying to solve. Here, at last, we reach the kernel of the international industrial marketer's role: to assemble the customer solutions from each market and to build the networks of SILK that will allow the local units to profit from the similarities.

# Services marketing[7]

George F. Brown, Jr, consulting group president at engineering firm ICF Kaiser International, emphasized that a business customer should be able to see how the services provided by its product vendors help it to serve its own customers. Specifically, five trends are reshaping business services marketing:

- The proliferation of services and service-surrounded products means that "Services are everywhere, and increasingly become part of the buyer's decision process," Dr Brown explained. "Services surrounding traditional products – finance, accounting, marketing, technology, research … the list goes on and on – are frequently becoming greater sources of profit and competitive advantage than the products themselves"

- Post-downsizing growth strategies cut customers' technical staffs, requiring that vendors perform the end user hand-holding a customer's own personnel once performed

- Wresting value from information and technology provides vendors with strong opportunities because customers might not yet realize the full value of their investments

- Globalization is unavoidable, putting pressure on vendors to be at least as global in their operations as their customers

- Public and private sector relationships, such as outsourcing, privatization, and public-private partnerships "are opportunities available to most businesses, particularly those that can play the same role in the public sector that they have in the private sector"

*Source:* Donath, B. (1996) "Delivering the value customers really want," *ISBM Insights*, 6(4). University Park, PA: Institute for the Study of Business Markets

Tangible products and intangible services are so regularly banded together that their marketing cannot, and should not, be divorced one from the other. Is a Burger King consumer buying a tangible product (the burger) or the fast service? Clearly both. The consumer could make better burgers at home or get faster service from an automat. The product and the service are wholly interdependent.

*The product and the service are wholly interdependent*

Technology is changing services marketing just as much as goods. ATMs are now preferred to counter clerks as a way to recover one's money from the bank. Some customers will wait in the rain to avoid personal service. Others enjoy the bank's ambience and relate to particular clerks. Service offers variety: there is no one "right" service for all, any more than there is a right-for-everyone physical good.

An assessment of a global brand, newly acquired in January 1989, revealed the following:

- 17 percent market share
- A management team that had not focused on profitability
- Total focus on operations at the expense of the customer
- Field structure dominated by "barons," which did not encourage co-ordination across the USA business
- Poorly co-ordinated international strategy
- Excellent products but no recent history of successful product introductions
- Lack of focus on the achievement of good management standards
- No check and balance between staff functions and operations
- An emphasis on controlling rather than supporting the field staff

*Source:* Internal report from a world-famous retail chain (identity necessarily concealed)

The problems in the above company, despite considerable management action, remained the same for several years to follow. Management was preoccupied by their sector being *different*. Expertise was bought and fired as reorganization followed reorganization. Initiative followed imperative. Until recently, no member of the executive committee stayed long enough to learn, or was prepared to learn.

As with any other sector, SILK (and animal spirits) provides the role of the international marketer of services. What then are the differences? Why do the Chinese, for instance, resist buying (and in particular, paying for) services when they are happy to buy physical goods? We crystallize two factors, which are not universal, but common enough to deserve special attention:

- The affective nature, but lack of standardization, inherent in people delivery systems
- The use of consumer time.

Expertise might be a third factor. We buy financial services, not so much to save time or because we are pleased by the service, but because we do not have the expertise to do it for ourselves. As marketers we are concerned with *brands*. A branded physical good provides us with expertise, in a sense, too. We could make a spade, perhaps, but it is quicker and cheaper to buy one that has been expertly made. Perhaps all products are really services; we do not buy the thing: we buy the services the thing does for us. For financial and professional services especially, we buy expertise. We also buy time. Perhaps we could complete our own tax returns but we prefer to buy the services of an accountant.

*All products are really services; we do not buy the thing: we buy the services the thing does for us*

The two inter-relate. We enjoy the emotional satisfaction of service when we have time and we make time for service situations we enjoy. Even so, it is simpler to take them separately.

## Service as affective satisfaction

Some researchers have taken the affective (emotional) nature of services satisfaction to extremes. Shopping (retail therapy) has been studied as compensation for sex.[8] The reciprocal theory, sex as compensation for unsatisfactory shopping experiences, has not yet received academic attention, so far as we know.

Sometimes services take the place of physical products. A remarkable marketing achievement is to charge customers more for *not* providing food, e.g. health spas. Premium prices, relative to hotels, are paid for deprivation that would have appalled Mother Teresa. From an aesthetic point of view, the customer gets a poor deal. He shares space with aged, overweight fellow sufferers shuffling about in bath robes. Of course, the premium gains access to, and/or reinforces membership of, a social group with similar values. Few maintain whatever physical benefit they gain, which enhances the probability of repeat sales. Great marketing!

More generally, we spend money to achieve the feel-good factor. The service brand marketer, therefore, has to be concerned with the whole service delivery experience. Marketing a film, or a political party, requires the measurement of the feel-good factor. The service clerk has an emotional relationship with the customer.[9] As noted in the opening of this chapter, one of the main sources of the relational perspective is services marketing.

The Ritz-Carlton's motto is simple: "Ladies and Gentlemen serving Ladies and Gentlemen." Its credo reinforces the emphasis on people and relationships:

The Ritz-Carlton Hotel is a place where the genuine care and comfort of our guests is our highest mission. We pledge to provide the finest personal service and facilities for our guests who will always enjoy warm, relaxed, yet refined ambience. The Ritz-Carlton experience enlivens the senses, instills well being, and fulfills even the unexpressed wishes and needs of our guests.

Their three steps of service are also aimed at "personalising" each guest's stay:
1   A warm and sincere greeting. Using the guest's name if and when possible
2   Anticipation and compliance with guest needs
3   Fond farewell. Give them a warm goodbye and use their names when and if possible

Source: Ritz-Carlton website (www.ritzcarlton.com/corporate/commitment.htm)

Empathy, the key to relational marketing, is highlighted in services and is difficult to transfer from market to market because:

- It is cultural. In some places even verbalizing these issues would be awkward.

- Affect cannot be expressed fully in cognitive terms, still less, measured reliably.

In New York, pleasure is taken and given by having one's shoes cleaned in public. In the UK, most people would find that embarrassing. Brand delivery by (unbrandable) people has advantages as well as risks for the international marketer. If local marketers fully understand and are committed to the global positioning strategy, then they are best placed to make the necessary cultural adaptation. Indeed, reinterpretation within the new cultural context should strengthen the positioning. One should not have to worry about putting an Indian "face" on the service product if it is delivered by an Indian. The matching risk is, of course, that understanding and commitment is missing. When locals adapt the brand on an NIH basis, they are likely to lose its very essence. In the 1970s, Hilton lost control of its brand positioning service varied excessively from place to place.

The best-known service quality model is that by Parasuraman, Zeithaml and Berry (PZB), which has been widely reproduced.[10] Essentially, it determines the consumer's "expected" service from past experience, personal needs and what they have heard about the brand. That is compared with management's perceptions of consumer expectations ("Gap 1"). Gap 1 is further analyzed into four other gaps between expectation and experience. Critics suggest the model replaces one unknown (service quality) by five. Furthermore, it depends on research in which consumers rationalize their feelings. We know this is unreliable.[11] Admirers claim it provides a measurement framework. It is also the best game in town.

### International services marketing

Whatever system is adopted, the international marketer needs *some* consistent service quality analysis so that metrics can be compared across borders. Previous chapters outlined the positioning → brand equity metrics process which the international and key national marketers should share. In services marketing, this should be extended to agreeing upon the best model of their particular service delivery from which consistent metrics can be deduced. Developing a shared model of customer satisfaction is the depth dimension of learning and planning. The PZB model is a good place to start, but feelings (A) should dominate cognition (C). This is reflected in new approaches under development.[12]

A few service marketing opportunities arise *because* of cross-border differences. Lionel Knight, of the Court Burkitt ad agency, tells of a US entrepreneur who spotted the Japanese wish to have the latest TV in their small homes in the 80s. This meant that they had to get rid of their existing set every 12–18 months. The entrepreneur charged a fee to pick up the "old" sets and sold them as nearly new on the US West Coast. The key was, that due to the phasing of the Japanese TV makers' international roll-outs, these nearly new sets were getting into US distribution at the same time as the launch of the new sets. A great outsight.

Consultants networked across the world can work round the clock on a problem transferred from each time zone to the next. The solutions can be back to clients in less than half the usual time. Similarly, satellites are globalizing media provision, both electronic and print. The impact of immediate information channels ripples through almost all services marketing across the globe. The globalization of information *channels* helps the harmonization of the information itself.

## International retail marketing

IKEA in the US is interesting for a number of reasons. Later in the article cited in the following case study, *The Economist* took IKEA to task because they had "cheerfully broken several rules of international retailing: enter a market only after exhaustive study, cater for local tastes as much as possible and gain local expertise through acquisition, joint ventures or franchising." IKEA had, in *The Economist*'s view, been lucky previously, "jumping into big new markets feet first."

Our research indicates that IKEA was right and the "rules" are not. Preserve existing differentiation when going in and then adapt when experience says you have to. Do not react to prior research. Existing tastes are based on existing buying habits, which are already catered for. Match those and existing competition will kill you. The moral of the American tale is that, despite consciously being a SILK company, IKEA learned too slowly from the US launch.

In 1985, IKEA opened a 15,700 sq m (169,000 sq ft) warehouse store outside Philadelphia. "At first, with the dollar at around SKr8.6, it was quite easy to make money," says Anders Moberg, IKEA's chief executive. Six more shops (five on the east coast and one in Los Angeles) followed in as many years.

But things had started to go wrong. By 1989 the American operation looked to be in deep trouble. In each new European country it entered, the company had broken into profit after two or three years with its third or fourth store. In America it was still losing money. And this could not be blamed wholly on a slowdown in the economy and a weak furniture market.

Many people visited the stores, looked at the furniture and left empty handed. Customers complained of long queues and constant non-availability of stock. Imitators were benefiting from the marketing effort IKEA had made in introducing Americans to Scandinavian design. Worst of all, since it was still making many of its products in Sweden, IKEA's cherished reputation for low-cost furniture was threatened as the dollar's value dropped to SKr5.8 by 1991.

Another retailer might, at that point, have sought a dignified exit. IKEA says it never considered that option. "If you're going to be the world's best furnishing company you have to show you can succeed in America, because there is so much to learn here," says Göran Carstedt, who took over North American operations four years ago.

*Source: The Economist, p. 101, 19 November 1994*

Marks & Spencer failed to match its UK success in Canada partly because it tried to adapt. The company got it right, eventually, in France, because it did not adapt. IKEA believes, likewise, in adapting its offering as little as possible. Going international does not require a change of consumer promise. Burger King is successful abroad because it is seen as American and makes few compromises with local tastes. Benetton sticks to the same formula world-wide.

Retail branding is growing in importance. Wal-Mart is going global. Gap may once have had a price positioning; today it sets its own style. The growth of retail branding, of course, puts retailers in competition with their suppliers. Some strongly branded retailers minimise the sales of other brands. That helps their differentiation. Others sell on price and *need* supplier brands in order to communicate their value message, Wal-Mart and Aldi (Germany) for example. Either way, the positioning of the retail brand has to be reinforced by the product portfolio.

Grocery retailing crosses borders with difficulty, unmatched by fast food restaurant brands. But the principle is the same: chain retailers now see their outlets as the packaging of their brands. Irrespective of their dependence on advertising, there is a determination to ensure that staff training, fascias, and layouts reflect the image the group is trying to communicate. In that pursuit, the role of store manager is pivotal for retail brand equity, so much so that the manager becomes a "customer" to be wooed and persuaded. The eternal triangle of marketing relationships (Figure 9.1) still applies. Unless the store manager understands, accepts and reinforces the mission of the chain, the chances of success are sharply reduced.

*The positioning of the retail brand has to be reinforced by the product portfolio*

Following that logic, HR or personnel departments began screening management trainees on the basis of "fit" with the required image. Critics think Marks & Spencer (M&S) recruits clones to be their managers and that their training intensifies this cloning. No doubt M&S disputes that. Do Andersen employees resemble each other or are "Androids" a myth created by competitors? Sainsbury became so conscious of the risks of sameness that they began recruiting deliberate misfits, but that, too, created problems. The business of branding people, or training them to present a standardized image, is full of traps.

Singapore Airlines attempted to solve the problem by hiring and training "Singapore Girls" to present a uniformly glamorous image to their customers, or the male customers at least. The "Girls" rebelled against this exploitative approach.

Retail staff turnover is typically high, wage levels and learning facility low. International consistency is difficult, even with training. Add empowerment, as Wal-Mart does, and the potential for divergence grows. International retail brand success requires attention to at least two factors:

- Deep understanding of the brand's positioning and metrics by every member of staff and especially the "boundary staff" who deal with customers.

- A strong IT spine, which takes care of whatever objective data and calculative processes that can be made routine. Integrated logistics with suppliers are hard to move across borders, but the electronic systems that enable them are another matter. In the US, Wal-Mart and Procter & Gamble initiated efficient consumer response (ECR) to cut waste from their systems in 1987. Years later, most European companies are still talking about it.

In the traditional shop, the personal relationship existed between the owner and the employees. They did not work for the store; they worked for the person. In the modern retail group, the CEO's personality, or even, name, may not be known to the store staff. Disney and its competitors train their staff as actors playing the roles the brands' customers expect to see.

Ben Schneider at the University of Maryland found that contented point-of-sale staff did not lead to contented customers.[13] On the other hand, where sales staff have a clear idea of their brand's positioning, and are rewarded for customer satisfaction, then the staff's perceptions of customer satisfaction, and that of the customers themselves, are very closely correlated. This is the P(urpose) of PASSION that reinforces performance.

To achieve a deep understanding of positioning, the customer marketing function needs to be integrated with the rest of the staff.[14] As long as the HR function is training one set of messages, and marketing communicating another, the customer will remain confused. The "brand," in the case of retail chains, with which the new employee is supposed to identify as paymaster, is the same "brand" that the employee is selling to customers. By adopting the brand as a single concept, training is simplified and made more powerful – especially with high-turnover, low-paid customer contact staff.

Employees respond to being treated as respected customers and customers want to feel part of the family, but few firms consider bringing marketing and HR into a single discipline. Improving the empathic relationship between point-of-sales staff and customers involves building between them the climate for social information. The context determines the extent. If your butcher is a member of your golf club, have you joined the wrong club or chosen the right butcher? Service is crucial and customer–staff relationships are built by empathic relationships, not Cartesian controls and logic.

## Marketing in the non-profit sector

To some extent, "non-profit" is a misnomer: all organizations must profit (though they may call it a "surplus") to survive. The key differences with other marketing sectors are:

- There is no single set of shareholders to satisfy financially.

- Stakeholders may be more diverse with different, even contrary, understandings of "success."

- Much of the strategic and administrative work, including marketing, is likely to be conducted by unpaid volunteers with little time and less patience. Even in a fully professional team, the resources available for marketing are likely to be even more stretched than in for-profit situations. Administration is the least popular funding objective.

> *To some extent, "non-profit" is a misnomer: all organizations must profit to survive*

- Two marketing plans are needed. One is comparable to other forms of marketing (how best to use resources to achieve the desired objectives) and the other is needed to raise the resources. Thus one plan looks forward (to end users) and one backwards (to those who supply the cash).

When a professional marketer is first engaged by a non-profit organization, the expectation is usually that they will simply gather in more money. Questioning the organization's reason for existence may be tolerated only for a while. The marketing role is seen as ancillary rather than fundamental. This is much less true in the USA where marketing has long played a major role in the development of the non-profit sector.

As in other sectors, international non-profit marketing involves cross-border learning, followed by planning, and begins with the product itself. These issues do not need further repetition.

The shared commercial orientation largely assumed in for-profit businesses will not exist in the non-profit sector. If funding is in crisis (it often is), consensus on objectives should lead to measures of success with two perspectives in mind: the "customers" who benefit from the non-profit's existence, and the donors. The two have to match. This lack of implicit consensus requires going backwards before moving forwards.

Inner-city youth work, for example, must win the support of those who need it as well as those who pay for it. Clarity of positioning, and notably differentiation, is central in much the same way as for any other brand. A US charity that innovated birth control in Bangladesh did not find acceptance by a culture that saw things differently. When the State decided to devote far greater resources to birth control, the role of the expatriate agency came into question. Rationally they should have been glad to have succeeded and closed up shop. M and A (of MAC) took over and they tried to expand the agency.

Marketing a non-profit organization to donors faces a classic catch-22 dilemma: money may be easier to raise where it is least needed. Sponsors want to be associated with success and with innovation. They like having their names associated with new capital projects. Providing running costs for charities in deficit has low appeal.

Going backwards (before continuing forwards) involves a fresh assessment of objectives and their mutual compatibility. This is likely to create a clash of paradigms. Members of the organization who have long done their own thing may be disturbed by discovering that colleagues see things differently. If the non-profit organization does not have a funding crisis, this stage may be postponed. Sooner or later, it will arise.

Once both sets (customer and donor) of objectives are clear, measures of success can be established and the business can move forward to the marketing plans. In non-profit organizations, non-financial measures will be relatively more important so far as the "customers" are concerned, whereas money income (turnover) remains the key measure for donor activity. The linkage of the two plans lies in the brand equity.

*The trump card for non-profit marketing is altruism*

Persuading those involved that brand equity measurement should take precedence over short-term cash is a challenge.

The trump card for non-profit marketing is altruism. Customers and donors know that the game is not being played for private gain. The market is just as competitive, perhaps more so, but at least the cause is seen as good.

International non-profit operations usually involve donors in richer countries transferring money to poorer; but it is not just money. The Bangladesh birth control agency had difficulty of raising money according to one set of ethics in one country and applying that in another where the culture was very different.

The Saxons were invited to live in Romania in the twelfth century and encouraged to leave over 800 years later. The many fine churches they left behind are maintained, with difficulty, with money raised in Germany. Romanian nationals see greater priorities for charity.

## Executive notes

- While diversity of experience and relationships may differ, the same basic frameworks apply to the business-to-business, services, retailing, and non-profit sector marketing

- The international marketer, more than ever, must be selective in the identification of end-user solutions, many of which can be gleaned from customers, and the cross-fertilization of knowledge and enthusiasm

- Despite similarities, a marketer in one sector cannot usually step into equal success in another

- Services, seen as affective transfer, depend upon point-of-sales staff in building the brand–customer relationship. A model is needed to measure these relationships and the Parasuraman, Zeithaml and Berry framework provides a starting point. But beware cognitive bias

- IT can be a central spine for the development of international service brands. Let the machine take care of the routine and calculative factors as well as much of the information storage. The mechanical parts of service businesses increasingly are being automated, e.g. ATMs

- Non-profit and industrial marketing follow usual consumer marketing principles but with greater complexity, e.g. customers and donors

# References

1. Yung, C. G. *Modern Man in Search of a Soul.*
2. The relational perspective of marketing from diverse disciplines, such as economics (Coase, 1937; Williamson, 1988), legal contracts (Macneil, 1978) and social psychology (Thibaut and Kelley, 1957; Caldwell, 1976), as well as different geographical regions, such as Scandinavia (Gronroos, 1990; Gummesson, 1987, 1993; Hakansson, 1982), the USA (Berry, 1983; Thorelli, 1964, 1986), and Australia (Ballantyne, 1994). The Fall 1983 special edition of the *Journal of Marketing* was given over to new marketing theory as alternatives to the traditional, dubbed "neoclassical," perspective (Arndt, 1983). These strands were brought together as "relationship marketing" (Gronroos, 1990; Christopher, Payne and Ballantyne, 1991; Parvatiyar and Sheth, 1994) and the "Relational Paradigm" (Wilson and Moller, 1991; Ambler, 1994). Distribution channels research has provided much of the relationship marketing literature (Anderson and Narus, 1991). The special issue of the *Journal of the Academy of Marketing Science* (Fall 1995) reflects diverse current thinking in the area.

Ambler, T. (1994) "The Relational Paradigm: A Synthesis" in Sheth, J. N. and Parvatiyar, A. (eds) (1994) *Research Conference Proceedings, Relationship Marketing: Theory, methods and applications*, June 11–13. Atlanta: Centre for Relationship Marketing, Emory University.

Anderson, J. and Narus, J. (1991) "Partnering as a Focused Market Strategy," *California Management Review*, Vol. 33 (Spring), pp. 95–113.

Arndt, J. (1983) "The Political Economy Paradigm: Foundation for theory building in marketing," *Journal of Marketing*, Vol. 47 (Fall), pp. 44–54.

Ballantyne, D. (1994) "Marketing at the Cross-roads," *Asia-Australia Marketing Journal*, Vol. 2(1), August, pp. 1–8.

Berry, L. L. (1983) "Relationship Marketing" in Berry, L. L. (ed) *Emerging Perspectives on Services Marketing*. Chicago: American Marketing Association, pp. 25–8.

Caldwell, M.D. (1976) "Communications and Sex Effects in a Five-Person Prisoner's Dilemma Game," *Journal of Personality and Social Psychology*, Vol. 27(1), pp. 38–49.

Christopher, M. *et al.* (1991) *Relationship Marketing. Bringing quality, customer service and marketing together*. Oxford: Butterworth-Heinemann.

Coase, R. H. (1937) "The Nature of the Firm," *Economica* NS4, pp. 386–405.

Gronroos, C. (1990) "Relationship Approach to Marketing in Service Contexts: The marketing and organizational behaviour interface" *Journal of Business Research* 20, pp. 3–11.

Gummesson, E. (1987) "The New Marketing – Developing Long-term Interactive Relationships," *Long Range Planning*, Vol. 20(4), pp. 10–20.

Hakansson, H. (1982) *Interactional Marketing and Purchasing of Industrial Goods: An interaction approach*. New York: Wiley.

Macneil, I. R. (1978) "Contracts: Adjustments of long-term economic relations under classical, neo-classical, and relational contract law," *Northwestern University Law Review*, Vol. 72, pp. 854–906.

Parvatiyar, A. and Sheth, J. N. (1994) "Paradigm Shift in Marketing Theory and Approach: The emergence of relationship marketing," in Sheth, J. N. and Parvatiyar, A. (eds) *1994 Research Conference Proceedings, Relationship Marketing: Theory, methods and applications*, June 11–13. Atlanta: Centre for Relationship

Marketing, Emory University.

Thibaut, J. W. and Kelley, H. H. (1959) *The Social Psychology of Groups*. New York: Wiley.

Thorelli, H. B. (1964) "Political Science and Marketing," in Cox, R. (ed) *et al*. *Theory in Marketing*. Homewood, IL: Richard D. Irwin, Inc., pp. 125–36.

Thorelli, H. B. (1986) "Networks: Between markets and hierarchies," *Strategic Management Journal*, (7), pp. 37–51.

Turnbull, P. W. (1987) "Interaction and International Marketing: An investment process," *International Marketing Review*, Vol. 4(4), pp. 7–19.

Williamson, O. (1988) "Discussion of 'Breach of Trust in Hostile Takeovers,'" in Auerbach, A. (ed) *Corporate Takeovers: Causes and consequences*, Chicago: University of Chicago Press.

Wilson, D. T. and Moller, K. K. E. (1991) "Buyer-Seller Relationships. Alternative Conceptualizations," in Paliwoda, S. J. (ed) *New Perspectives on International Marketing*. London: Routledge, Chapter 5, pp. 87–107.

3. Hutt, M. D. and Speh, T. W. (1989) *Business Marketing Management*. 3rd edn. New York: The Dryden Press, p. 11.

4. Williamson, O. (1985) *The Economic Institutions of Capitalism*. New York and London: The Free Press.

5. Dr Baker spent 28 years with Shell in both technical and commercial roles. Since 1984, he has consulted on US market entry for European high technology products.

6. Von Hippel, E. (1988) *The Sources of Innovation*. Oxford: Oxford University Press, p. 15.

7. For a complete coverage of services marketing, *see* Lovelock, C. (1996) *Services Marketing*. 3rd edn. Upper Saddle River, NJ: Prentice Hall; and its recent country-specific adaption: Lovelock, C. *et al*. (1998) *Services Marketing: Australia and New Zealand*. Sydney: Prentice Hall (Australia).

8. Woodruffe, H. R. *et al*. (1997) "Better Than Sex? Exploring Shopping as Compensatory Behaviour," *Proceedings of the Academy of Marketing*. Manchester, July.

9. Grayson, K. (1998) "Customer Responses to Emotional Labour in Discrete and Relational Service Exchange," *International Journal or Service Industry Management*, Vol 9 (2), pp. 126–54.

10. Parasuraman, A., Zeithaml, V. and Berry, L. (1985) "A Conceptual Model of Service Quality and its Implications for Future Research," *Journal of Marketing*, Fall, p. 44.
Reproduced in, for example, Kotler, P. (1997) *Marketing Management*. 9th edn. Upper Saddle River, NJ: Prentice Hall, p. 478.

11. Wilson, T. D. *et al*. (1989) "Introspection, Attitude Change, and Attitude-Behavior Consistency: The disruptive effects of explaining why we feel the way we do," *Advances in Experimental Social Psychology*, Academic Press, 22, pp. 287–343.

12. Edwardson, M. (1998) "Measuring Consumer Emotions in Service Encounters: An exploratory analysis," *Australasian Journal of Market Research*, Vol. 6, 2, pp. 34–48.

13. Schneider, B. and Bowen, D. E. (1993) "The Service Organization: Human resources management is crucial," *Organizational Dynamics*, Vol. 21(4), Spring, pp. 39–52.

14. Ambler, T. and Barrow, S. (1996) "The Employer Brand," *The Journal of Brand Management*, Vol. 4, 3 (December), pp. 185–206.

# chapter 10

# Digital relationships

'Yet even if e-mail does bring about deep and subtle changes
in organizational life, it will soon seem the most
prosaic medium for corporate communication'

*Source:* R. McKenna[1]

---

Today when Paula Smith, of Portland, Oregon, goes to a book shop, she grabs a shopping cart, wanders through the aisles and glances through some new releases in the reading room. She also finds an interview with a new author. Paula then searches through the 2.5 million listings, by title, author, subject, keyword, and ISBN number. After finding the books she wants, Paula goes to the check-out and pays. Before leaving, she asks to be notified when her favorite author releases his next book. Swee Tiong Tan, in Singapore, visited the same shop this morning. Neither customer had left home. They were both visiting www.amazon.com – Earth's biggest bookstore.

---

To what extent do e-commerce, the World Wide Web, the magic of fax, e-mail, voice-mail, and video conferencing, change the fundamental chemistry of marketing and how businesses add value? Since information technology does not excuse the international marketer seeking social information from wide travel, and digital wonders cannot spark animal spirits, are they not reduced to bean counters and picture toys? What is their place in developing a SILK culture of experiential learning?

While forecasts of paperless offices are not worth the paper they are written on, information technology does profoundly change traditional dimensions of time, space, and communications.[2]

*Executives are operational wherever they may be: electronic channels change the very concept of "away"*

Consumers, as well as executives, want and receive instant gratification anywhere and at any time. The pace of life quickens and simplifies. Wherever in the world and whatever time of night, the international executive can plug in his laptop, tune in his palmtop, and enter his virtual office. The extent to which that allows him to operate outside conventional place and time has been a recurring theme. Indeed, executives are operational wherever they may be: electronic channels change the very concept of "away."

Information technology does not *replace* traditional media for doing business in old ways: it *adds* new media, which allows new ways of doing business. Electronic commerce (e-commerce) covers a wide range of business activity: Web shopping, stock and bond transactions, buying/downloading software, and business networks that co-ordinate purchasing, inventory control and payments. Forrester Research estimated $7 billion of online consumer transactions by the year 2000, while business-to-business transactions were expected to hit $66 billion by that time.[3] General Electric already does $1 billion worth of business through its Trading Process Network website.

Other estimates, for North America and Europe, suggest the following online percentages of total e-commerce sales by 2010:[4]

- 60 percent for retail, banks, travel agents, airlines and mail-order clothing firms
- 30 percent for music, books and newspapers
- 15 percent for groceries
- 10 percent for cars and white goods.

Here we review briefly how the Web will change marketing; building digital relationships with channel members; the role of e-commerce in developing brand–consumer relationships; the use of e-commerce in going international and the digital impact on international marketers. We have included this chapter, not because the world is short of introductions to the Web, but because it destroys borders. Just clicking a mouse can carry the international consumer across sectors, national borders, space and even, in a sense, time.

## The Web's effect on marketing

Great advances in technology do not fundamentally change the basic needs of customers. Convenience and the need to stay in touch were desired by customers long before mobile phones were invented. However, technology does present marketers with new and often better ways of serving these needs. Technology can also change – and substantially raise – customer expectations with respect to service, product quality, delivery times and so on.

*The Web is reducing distance and time to the here and now*

The digital age that is unfolding on our screens has already had profound effects on the way we relate to each other, our customers, and business partners. The frequency of communication with friends across the globe has dramatically increased and the nature of that communication has changed. Why? Primarily because it is easy, cheap and happening in real time. The Web, more than satellite TV, more than anything, is reducing distance and time to the here and now.

### Segmentation

The principle of dividing a market into different sub-groups or market segments was introduced by the economist Wendell Smith in 1956.[5] Simply put, different groups of consumers have different needs and profiles, and each, therefore, requires a tailored marketing program. We have the mass market at one end of the spectrum and individual consumers at the other. The process of segmentation involves the grouping of consumers in appropriate and profitable ways. The digital age has made the segment of one individual not only feasible, but increasingly essential. Why should a customer respond to a "Dear Sir/Madam" letter from their bank when their supermarket is able to personalize offers according to their particular pattern of weekly purchases? Since we experience personalized service in some areas, we expect it everywhere. Thus the digital revolution is radically changing expectations.

In practice, segmentation has been a mixed blessing. In terms of focussing more specifically on the true target market, the analysis has been all good. On the other hand, targeting many segments independently multiplies the marketing effort as many times as there are segments. Using information technology to streamline marketing planning and implementation, and using the Web to deliver, may help.

## Communication

"Webvertising" has the potential to be truly interactive. First, if consumers decide they want to engage in communication, they double click their mice. The potential customer can be led to a site, but they may also choose whether to stay, or continue surfing in another direction. This should be two-way communication that the consumer largely controls, dictating both the direction and speed of the communication. Few "Webvertisers" have yet mastered the techniques of *listening* to consumer input, except in the most mechanical ways. As technologies converge, they will improve. But consumers are unlikely to forget the difference between speaking with a person and a computer. They will need both services. Remember also that there are some times when, after a hard day of interacting with people and machines, we are quite happy to put our feet up and be passive "viewers." The old will sit comfortably with the new.

## Product design

In the industrial mind-set, manufacturers make products, sometimes with the aid of consumer research, ship them off to retailers (their direct customers), and hope that their advertising to consumers will convince buyers to empty the retail shelves. But, will the products be exactly what the consumer really wants/needs? How do the manufacturer and retailer manage inventory – particularly when a number of product variations are involved – and how long will it take the system to react if consumers do not buy? Dell Computer Corporation does not share these problems. The consumer comes to the site and builds the machine to their own specifications. Dell maintains minimal inventory. For orders from Australia, the product is built in Malaysia and shipped to the Australian home address within a week. Why should buying a car be any different? (*See* the following for some speculation.) Take a look at Ford's website (www.ford.com) and see the future; but they had better hurry: Dell has already identified the high costs of inventory and dealerships in the car market and is planning to get involved.

In 2020, buyers of passenger vehicles could order their products in one of two ways. The first will be to go into an interactive showroom. At these showrooms customers will be able to see and drive a select number of prototypes of a particular brand. Then they will sit down with a design consultant, a PC and virtual reality equipment, and "build" their car on screen. They will be able to select colours, features and any special requirements that they want tailor-made. Once this is finished, the order will be placed by e-mailing it to a clearing centre. The software that will receive the design will translate it into the required components and the most efficient assembly process. Within 48 hours suppliers will have shipped the components, partially assembled, to a central assembly centre that will be supervised, although perhaps not owned, by the manufacturer. Final assembly and quality control would take place and the car would be delivered to the customer's house about a week from the initial order.

More sophisticated customers will design their car on their own, using a website. Virtual reality "helmets" and other devices will help customers get a better feel for what they are buying. With this technology, their car will be ordered and delivered just like their groceries.

Commercial vehicles – light trucks etc. – will be designed by the sellers and buyers, using similar interactive software as the consumer market. Customisation will not be a selling point but the price of being in business. Competition will be based on innovation, the range of features available, speed and value.

The sellers of these vehicles will be the hubs of supplier networks. Their main role will be to put together these networks of designers, suppliers and sub-assemblers, and then manage the logistics of marketing and delivery. They will all be out to create the "lifetime" customer, through strong brands, service delivery and financial products. Managing and motivating the network of relationships will be their primary role, with service as the key.

The leaders in this new world could be Korea. The Americans and Ford gave us mass production, Toyota gave us quality and efficiency, but it could be Korea, through companies like Hyundai and Daewoo, that will give us the disposable "Swatch" type car.

*Source:* Styles, C. "The Mayflower Decision," unpublished case study
(with thanks to PricewaterhouseCoopers)

## Pricing

Pricing for CDs, like books, has become global. If taxes are the reason "local" prices are high, then governments beware! The Web is watching. Companies like US-based PriceScan and Esmarts.com trawl websites and paper catalogues to create up-to-the-minute databases that help customers find the lowest price available. These price watchdogs cover everything from computing equipment to toys.

Global auction markets continue to grow, whether for airline tickets or cameras. Priceline.com, based in the US, for example, allows potential passengers to name their price for a trip between two cities – if an airline accepts the price, the customer must buy. eBay, a more generalised auctioneer with more than 1,000 categories available, receives 140 million hits a week. Bargaining will no longer be confined to the clothing stalls of Bangkok or the used car dealer. Research by Jupiter Communications suggests online business-to-consumer auctions will be worth $3.2 billion annually by 2002. That will come from 6.5 million consumers (up from 1.2 in 1998) – 11 percent of the total online shopping population.

## Distribution

Traditional retailing has the consumer coming to the store to choose, buy, and collect goods. The Web allows all three to be done without the customer leaving home. In cash-rich, time-poor societies, such as the US, this has to be a winner. It also dramatically changes the nature of distribution economics as well as the set of skills and abilities that marketing organizations will need. Store layout becomes a matter of Web design, inventory selection disappears, and full coverage is required. Building adequate parking lots is replaced by a more difficult challenge – the global delivery of goods from source to the customer's door at minimal cost. From the global marketer's viewpoint, physical becomes increasingly irrelevant as "market space" replaces "market-place" in the distribution lexicon. As long as consumers receive the goods in a few days, or overnight, they care little where they came from.

# Building digital relationships with channel members

An early (1980s) application of e-commerce was electronic data interchange (EDI). EDI uses networked computer systems to connect all parts of the value chain; for example, suppliers, wholesalers and retailers. The goal was a uniform electronic format to simplify communications through use of a common business language. Reels of magnetic tape were soon replaced by computer networks in a drive to reduce the waste and inefficiencies involved in inventory control, ordering, shipping and invoicing.

Wal-Mart was one of the major developers of these systems. Information technology, including electronic point of sale (EPOS) tills, provides data for detailed understanding of customers' habits and preferences. Real-time inventory data, along with intelligent learning systems that predict demand, network directly with supplier systems to drive production and deliveries. This reduces warehousing and data processing costs, e.g. using 10 percent of space for storage versus the 25 percent average of competitors.[6] General Motors, Ford, Rover and Chrysler have used EDI to reduce the number of suppliers and improve efficiency.

In consumer goods, EDI has played a critical role in the efficient consumer response (ECR) movement. The ECR Europe executive board expresses its vision as "working together to fulfil consumer wishes better, faster, and at less cost."[7] The board has 18 members, divided equally between retailers and manufacturers, including Tesco, Safeway, Unilever, Procter & Gamble, Metro/Asko and Nestlé. In 1996 Coopers & Lybrand estimated that implementing ECR in Europe would result in significant cost savings, estimated to equate to a 5.7 percent reduction in consumer prices for the average business in the grocery supply chain. The company believed it would be achieved through eight areas where waste could be reduced:

• Scanning accuracy

• Store ordering

• Continuous replenishment

• Optimized promotions

• Assortment planning, i.e. getting the best mix of SKUs (stock keeping units)

• Operational reliability

- Synchronizing production
- Integration with suppliers.

ECR has been difficult to implement because of ingrained attitudes and old-fashioned "turf" warfare. There has been resistance to massive changes in logistics. The shift in ECR is from competition to co-operation, both with customers/suppliers and immediate competitors. The electronic networks require common standards for everything from product codes to protocols. The technology thus summons all parties to spend less time fighting over the pie, and more time working in partnership to expand the pie. This is not the easiest cultural shift to negotiate.

Golden Cat Corporation uses software to help predict sales, taking into consideration promotions, bad weather, and numerous other variables. It also provides for continuous replenishment. This system cannot happen without EDI, which includes data swaps with key retailers. The result is that all mail and fax orders have been eliminated. Golden Cat wanted to help themselves deliver the best product to the consumer and help retailers make more money. In one supermarket, with $4 million in cat litter sales, category profits doubled to 4.9 percent following the changes. They changed the mix of items, cut the number of SKUs held, ran just-in-time delivery of inventory, and sold product before it was paid for. Internally, Golden Cat now has retail sales teams comprising individuals from different functions (logistics, sales, marketing). Key to this outcome is the interpretation of the information that was already available to supermarket management. Previously they did not have the resources to analyse it nor communicate the conclusions to their suppliers. By using the supplier specialists as part of their team to review the information and consider alternative formats, the information could be translated into actions for both supermarkets and suppliers. At the same time, those results guided the suppliers toward more effective management tools, i.e. information synchronised with their customers' management information. Golden Cat now plans promotions and merchandising six months ahead, working from the same side of the desk as the retailers. Retailers now focus on selling well rather than buying well, i.e. pulling consumers into the store rather than pushing the merchandising onto the shelves.

*Source:* Liesse, J. (1994) "The Nitty Gritty of ECR Systems: How one company makes it pay," *Advertising Age* (65, 19), Chicago, 99.S1–S3

Part of the growth of the internet can be attributed to the Web, allowing even the smallest firms to climb aboard the EDI bandwagon. The growth of the Internet has been, and still is, dramatic. eStats estimates that the number of Internet users will nearly quadruple from 36 million in 1997 to 142 million in 2002, an annual growth rate of 79 percent. They also estimate that revenues from e-commerce in the US alone will jump from $20 billion to $300 billion, over the same period.

## Developing brand–consumer relationships

Although constantly changing its look and content, the Lexus Automobile website (it was called the "Center for the Performance Art") was set up to develop new, and build existing, customer relationships. The website allows potential customers to "interact" with the brand before purchase, gathering information about alternative models, finance packages and new versus used car options. The site's section on the sporting and cultural events, sponsored by Lexus, helps to establish the brand's personality. Through their interactive experience with the site, customers are able to decide whether or not they want to associate with the Lexus brand – much as they might when first meeting someone. If they purchase a Lexus, the site allows them to enter "owner-only" sites. This kind of website helps both the brand and the customer deepen their relationship with each other, i.e. reinforcing the customer's purchase behavior, and allowing the brand to gather more information about the customer.

By combining EDI and Internet technology, business-to-business marketers maintain relationships on a fully automated basis. Dell Computer Corporation uses dedicated websites for its larger commercial customers, such as Boeing (which is thought to buy approximately 1,000 PCs each week). A range of information about the preferences and needs of these customers is built into Dell's electronic systems, which can be used world-wide by any company subsidiary. This technique helps a company reduce inventory and the risks associated with rapid obsolescence. Combined with the elimination of the wholesale/retail intermediary, this reduces costs substantially.

Intermediaries are not obsolete – their role is changing. In many ways, Dell is operating as an intermediary – between PC component manufacturers and end users. Dell adds value by providing the infrastructure that translates customer needs into product solutions, which are priced attractively and delivered efficiently. Boeing trusts Dell to understand what it needs, choose the right component suppliers, assemble the PCs, deliver them on time, and service the product after purchase.

Other business applications include:[8]

## Yellow pages

Merchants pay providers for placing information about them in an organized, searchable database. Users search this information without charge. This type of model can be implemented in a database format, such as the Catalog Mart Home Page, or as a "virtual mall" (a collection of storefronts under different categories of goods), such as eMall.

## Web traffic control

An advertisement that attracts a potential customer to a commercial site. Once there, the surfer finds the content may be transitory, offer incentives, or take the form of a "public service announcement." For example, "Lucky Leprechaun's Lane" is actually a site for finding apartments.

## Online storefront

The historic importance of shopfront design is based on its role as display advertising. Single websites, such as Amazon bookshop, are virtual shops as well as advertisements. Customers may use paper to place orders, but e-mail, e-fax, or using toll-free telephone numbers are encouraged. In due course, credit cards will be replaced by e-cash.

## Standard website

An internet presence for a brand may be in the form of a flat ad (which could just as easily appear in a magazine), an image site, which has emotional appeal to consumers, or a site that simply aims to provide information. Some car manufacturers, e.g. Mercedes, BMW, Volvo, and Mazda, originally took this option. More typically, the site is interactive, encouraging the surfer to explore the ideas and information behind the leading page and thus build the brand–consumer relationship. To do this, the advertiser has to provide involvement through interactive games or novelties. Passive reading is better provided in print.

## Content sites

These sites can be fee-based, where the user pays for access to content, or sponsored, whereby editorial content is supported by a variety of "advertisers." An example of a fee-based site is Encyclopaedia Britannica, and of a sponsored site is Global News Navigator. Community sites are fast-growing forms. One of the most successful, found at www.parentsplace.com, features articles on parenting with chat sites where participants can discuss problems and give advice. Not surprisingly, this site is heavily sponsored by manufacturers of baby and child products.

These e-tools fit the different stages of relationship development, and dimensions (*see* Table 10.1).

**Table 10.1 – Electronic solutions to relationship building**

| Relationship stage | Characteristics | E-commerce solutions |
|---|---|---|
| Awareness | • Proximity<br>• Perceive the potential for a relationship | • Search engines<br>• Yellow pages/Web traffic control sites |
| Exploration | • Interaction<br>• Information<br>• Opportunity for trial | • Storefront/internet presence sites<br>• Limited time trial sites (for information/data products) |
| Expansion | • Atmosphere of trust<br>• Mutual dependence<br>• High degree of risk-taking | • E-mail as a channel for customer feedback<br>• Secure payment systems<br>• Facility to return products<br>• Online after sales service<br>• Opportunity for EDI |
| Commitment | • Continuity in the relationship<br>• High level of inputs by both parties | • Ongoing EDI links<br>• Special privilege websites |

The growing number of portals, which includes Yahoo!, CNN.com and most internet service providers (ISPs), signals the importance of brands and brand equity in the cyberworld. Competition to be the "home page" on

*The growing number of portals signals the importance of brands and brand equity in the cyberworld*

your browser is intense – witness the offers of free e-mail and other services. By being a user's first port of call on the internet, a portal can stake claim to the primary relationship with its customers. It attempts to bring together the best collection of news, general interest and other content sites on behalf of its customers, and in doing so becomes the gateway and filter for advertising. The portals, content providers, advertisers and users have much to gain by building these relational networks.

While e-commerce provides new ways to build relationships, it also provides new ways to alienate existing and potential customers. Stupid menus, obscure paths, and complex jargon are but a few of the problems. Huge claims are made for one-to-one dealing, customization, and two-way communications that cannot be delivered *en masse*. In pilot studies they are fine and in practice they work, so long as they remain the province of the few.

Trust is double-edged. If the "brand" needs to understand the consumer, a great deal of personal information is required. At least initially, the consumer has neither the time, the interest, nor the trust in the "brand" to supply the data. The "brand," therefore, must not offer inappropriate menus and generalised offerings, which irritate the consumer.

Australian customers show a marked reluctance to embrace internet banking. A 1999 survey by PricewaterhouseCoopers found consumer attitudes to online banking marked by suspicion, ignorance and indifference. Those who professed Internet sophistication were still highly circumspect about providing personal details over the net. They feared a deluge of junk mail would result. In general, the survey indicated that banks need to win customers' trust before they can woo them online. Three-quarters of those surveyed said they would need to know the bank well before they would feel comfortable using its service online. Two-thirds added they would not be comfortable if particular financial products were offered only online and not also through traditional channels.

Building a consumer database, while respecting these sensitivities, requires more sophistication than most firms yet deploy. The considerations we suggest are little different from those normally used in gaining familiarization with another:

- Ask few questions. Collect a very small amount of new information non-intrusively at each contact opportunity.

- Draw knowledge from consumer behavior, e.g. purchases.

- Provide all possible media, e.g. mail, phone, personal visit, e-mail, and ensure that all channels lead to the same, single file.

- Do not flaunt your knowledge and surprise the consumer. This is a subtle issue of intrusiveness. For example, if you have once stayed at a hotel, you will be pleased they remember you and do not ask your address on your next visit. But, if they have all your data from another hotel, you may think less of that second hotel. Computer gossip is as dangerous as any other kind.

- Being careful, as above, fill gaps in the database until hard data is available by drawing inferences from the data you do have. For example, the home address provides some clues about wealth and lifestyle; intelligent systems can do this work.

- Explain how privacy is protected. Do not provide customer data to others. Asking if you may share this data or, worse still, saying that you will unless they indicate otherwise, damages trust. Selling lists is not worth the harm to brand equity.

The "para-social" relationship between brand and consumer is built in very much the same way as normal social relationships. So far, managers or call centers and relational databases have been extraordinarily inept. Mistakes can usually be avoided so long as the system designer empathizes with the consumer at each stage.

## Born global

With the Web, the era of the "born global" marketer has arrived. Information technology provides new opportunities for even the most novice of exporters and success depends on individual imagination. Technology is no longer a barrier. The slow country-by-country development can now be accelerated. Here are three ways firms are using the Web in international marketing.

### Profile of international companies

Setting up an efficient, professional website that instantly makes a firm global may cost $15,000 (with a range from $500 to $500,000), although ongoing costs can be quite substantial. Combined with EDI software, small companies *can* become part of large international value chains and trading networks. Without great ingenuity, however, they are more likely to be lost among millions of other sites. Search engines find big companies first and big companies have large attractive sites.

### Identifying potential partners

While websites and e-mail addresses give access to the globe, many firms will first choose to develop a single foreign market. It is no longer necessary to use a local consultant or embassy to list potential distributors. Databases can be accessed from the home office. Export promotion agencies and brokers provide online databases to help partners find each other. In addition, initial market research can be done quickly and efficiently using the wealth of commercial information available on the Web. For example, the UK Department of Trade and Industry's website provides detailed information (market structure etc.) about various industry sectors within a range of countries. New market entrants can also use the Web to help plan market visits, in terms of where they should go, and who they should meet.

### Product and service offerings

Opportunities exist for both standardization and customization.[9] The Dell Computer example demonstrates how electronic tools can allow customers to design their own products. A start-up Australian fund management company sells trust units to residents in Switzerland, which outperform the market by 10 percent. EDI streamlines and simplifies business paperwork. Use famous brands, e.g. VISA, to certify the legitimacy of your product.

As mentioned earlier, e-mail is not a medium for creating new relationships (although it may provide an initial contact point and spark of interest), and IT does not replace the basics of going international. On the other hand, e-commerce provides useful extras for the small business going international for the first time.

# The digital impact on international marketers

All in all, e-commerce is good for global marketing. It allows domestic firms to internationalize more quickly and at less cost. It allows international firms to communicate internally and externally with greater efficiency. Fax replaced telex, which, in turn, replaced the telegram. But e-mail is only partly replacing mail, fax and phone. It is better seen as a different, more informal medium than fax and more convenient than phone. For networking purposes, e-mail is easily copied and relayed, though excess should be avoided. Many of us have learned to screen out e-mails addressed to multiple recipients.

Above all, e-mail can nurture, but cannot create, the long-term relationships so crucial to international marketing. The decision by Boeing to enter into an automated relationship with Dell was not made by two machines, but by personal contact between executives on both sides. The success of the P&G/Wal-Mart relationship rests with the personal relationships and interactions between P&G's key account team and Wal-Mart's buyers. Although non-Thais can learn a great deal about Thailand from the internet, they can never really understand Thai consumers, the way they do business and their feelings towards products, unless they interact directly. Understanding culture requires personal experiential learning, the wellspring of social information.

*E-mail can nurture, but cannot create, the long-term relationships so crucial to international marketing*

What, then, is the place of information technology (IT) in terms of Social Information, Learning and Knowledge (SILK)? Bear in mind the primary goal in SILK is the conversion of implicit information into explicit value through experiential learning. "Outsights" and metaphor precede analytic reasoning.

We do not presume to forecast all possible uses of e-commerce, e-mail, broadband communications, or the wider wonders of the full IT menagerie. However, three opportunities are open to marketers to save time and nurture relationships:

- Routine information gathering should be computerized, releasing *time* to search for social information and outsights. International marketers once had to reprocess information from national units both for themselves and for headquarters. Smart companies today have removed e-boundaries between internal databases so that all marketers now share international data warehouses. The number of secretaries and clerical support staff in a large international marketing department, for example, has typically dwindled to one sole assistant to provide a human voice for callers. Most of the routine communications traffic are voice-mail and e-mail. Similarly, if business processes and brand–consumer relationship building have become electronic at the national level, executives should be more available to share development and experiences from other countries

- Video-conferencing allows new visual creative work to be agreed upon from a *distance*, body language to be interpreted, and many of the implicit aspects of social information to come into place, which previously were only possible through personal visits

- Planning is *learning* and the formal parts of planning can be lodged in cyberspace without any need for paper. A global company plan is a neutral, *n*-dimensional worksheet that matches the formal structure of the organization. The dimensions are the business unit, types of income and expense (account codes), time (months) and any others determined by the nature of the matrix structure. Security will dictate who can inspect and who can change which parts of the "cyberplan" but, in principle, anyone can participate online in rehearsing the next year's corporate reality, at any time of day and wherever they may be located. Few firms have taken this learning concept so far but the opportunity for global learning through global planning exists

One final caveat: knowledge is the permanent residue of experience, of which databases are a small part. Today's chief knowledge officers (CKOs) amass, share, and protect corporate knowledge.[10] The logic is obvious: computers have more reliable memories than executives and they walk out the door less often. In practice, the largest part of a CKO's job is to create a culture in which national executives will *want* to centralize information and will *want* to enquire about information they need. No amount of digitalization will bring a demand for learning.

*Computers have more reliable memories than executives and they walk out the door less often*

# Executive notes

- The Web is an ultimate boundary remover

- Information technology has, and will continue to have, a profound effect on global marketing, particularly communications and distribution

- Electronic communications can develop and strengthen relationships, both between suppliers and customers, and between brands and customers, at different stages of the progression. E-commerce will create more competition, often from unexpected sources. Customers will be able to play a greater part in creating their own products (mass customization)

- Marketers are well placed to enjoy the impact of e-commerce on all aspects of their functions, from consumer relationships to innovation and marketing plans, both nationally and globally

- Electronic media do not replace, so much as supplement, SILK. Corporate knowledge will be amassed, shared, and protected in more formal ways, but will remain merely the final, rather than the driving, stages of PASSION and performance

# References

1. McKenna, R. (1997) *Real Time: Preparing for the age of the never satisfied customer.* Boston, Massachusetts: Harvard Business School Press, p. 116.
2. McKenna, R. *ibid.*
3. Quoted at http://www.cnet.com/Content/Builder/Business/Ecommerce20/ss08.html.
4. London Business School Future Media Project estimates.
5. Smith, W. (1956) "Product differentiation and market differentiation as alternative marketing strategies," *Journal of Marketing*, July, pp. 3–8.
6. Koselka, R. (1992) "Distribution Revolution," *Forbes*, 25 May, pp. 54–62.
7. Coopers & Lybrand (1996) "Efficient Consumer Response – Europe," *First Official Conference of ECR Europe*, Geneva, 25–26 January.
8. Hoffman, D. L. *et al.* (1995) "Commercial Scenarios for the Web: Opportunities & challenges," *Journal of Computer-mediated Communication*, 1(3).
9. Quelch, J. A. and Klein, L. R. (1996) "The Internet and International Marketing," *Sloan Management Review*, Spring, pp. 60–75.
10. Earl, M. J. and Scott, I. A. (1999) "What is a Chief Knowledge Officer?," *Sloan Management Review*, Winter, pp. 29–38.

# chapter

# 11

# Connectivity for the global marketer

'Personal relations are the most important thing for ever and ever,
and not this outer life of telegrams and anger'

*Source:* E. M. Forster[1]

We now know some of the secrets behind the genius of Albert Einstein, thanks to a study of his brain lead by Dr Sandra Witelson, a neuroscientist at McMaster University in Hamilton, Canada. It seems that his brain was different from a "normal" brain in two ways. First, the two areas of the brain involved in the generation and manipulation of spatial images were 1 cm larger, giving 15 percent extra capacity. This may explain why Einstein described the way he thought as not in words, but as "associative play" or "more or less clear images." (To help him develop the theory of relativity he imagined himself as a "man in a box" travelling through the universe on a ray of light.) The second difference was that it did not have one of the deep grooves that usually separates one part of the brain from another. As a result, it is likely that more neurons could establish connections (i.e. communicate) with each other, making it possible for his brain to reach conclusions that other brains could not.

This suggests that differences in people's ability to think may be partly explained by physical differences in the brain. So can we alter this physical make-up and all become (or design our children to become) as brilliant as Einstein? In a recent study, scientists bred strains of mice with extra copies of a gene coded for a protein that can facilitate communications between neurons.[2]

Like Einstein, these mice make associations more easily and create more memories than normal mice. While this biochemical intervention won't itself make them more intelligent, it will allow the adult mice to retain a neural openness for learning that young mice naturally possess, but lose in ageing. If, as it is likely, that this can be replicated in humans, it will mean that the combination of more "connector" genes, plus greater opportunities to make connections (i.e. opportunities for learning), may make coming up with another theory of relativity child's play.

---

Finally we lengthen our lens to see the future environment for global international business. The old order will not die away. Narrowcasting will supplement, not replace, broadcasting. Thus life will become even more complex and the pressures to simplify will increase. That means that brands will become more important.

There are five radical connectivity shifts which concern us:

- The machine age, which began with Watt and his kin a quarter millennium ago, is giving way to the biological age. Our fascination with machinery, which fashioned the way we understood change, is switching to a biological perspective as we see the world, and organizations, as living systems. Of course, machinery will continue to grow in sophistication and application, but the more exciting developments will be organic.

- Distance and time differences are disappearing. We can digitally connect with anyone, at any time, from wherever we are. For the international marketer too, these barriers are reducing.

- Digitizing explicit communication will renew the attention given to the implicit. Place a tape recorder near a dinner party of six people, all interacting and enjoying themselves. The words strung together will make little sense to one not present during the party: sentences begin but do not finish, yet each member of the party understands the other perfectly.

- New Structures. Formal organigrams are giving way to networks of individuals working together because they want to, because they share commitment to solving a joint problem.

- Post-Cartesianism. Just as the machine will continue to develop, even as it fades from center stage, the rational, and the cognitive will also grow. Post-modernism expresses the desire to move beyond the confines of narrow logic, but has provided little in its place. The Memory Affect Cognition sequence brings feelings center stage.

All these trends may be seen as one: they are all consequences of the arrival of the ultimate machine: the computer. This chapter's opening case study shows that even our ability to think depends on connectivity and our open-ness to learning. Today's computers think, in a manner of speaking, but lack self-consciousness, emotion and life. Big Blue may perform stunning chess moves, processing algorithms at amazing speeds. However, the computer doesn't "'know" anything in the sense of mind–body knowing. Computers do not spark social information or process the implicit. Molecular nanotechnology may, some day, build biological computers with souls. That will pose enormous ethical and philosophical problems. Meanwhile, the divide is clear. Descartes was anticipating the age of enlightenment. Then it was: "I think, therefore I am." The biological age will be more sentient: "I feel, therefore I am."

*Today's computers think, in a manner of speaking, but lack self-consciousness, emotion and life*

## The biological age

More attuned to a biological view of marketing and organizations than we are, our successors may feel sorry for the twentieth century use of second-hand body parts, just as we feel sorry for those who can only afford second-hand clothes. Today we use other people's blood and organs. In most countries, they are freely given and received. Some have commercialized the traffic; others find the practice distasteful. Today we can grow spare parts from our own tissue and DNA. Scientists inject human brain cells into mice and they adapt into mouse brains. It will not be long before younger versions of our own brain cells are available for our own use. As the ability to grow new body parts increases, and spare money in health services declines, brain and body parts' replacement will be put on a commercial footing. How else can R&D be funded?

A US manufacturer now reconstitutes bovine bones into various formats for human use. With all the Mad Cow hysteria, it is surprising that the use of bovine material in this way is completely unregulated in the UK (1998). Not for long. The bone-making firms can afford only to market their goods for profit, as do false teeth manufacturers. New skin is grown from single cells on a non-profit basis but only because the process is cheap.

Just as we would now be appalled by having someone else's teeth when we could have new dentures, we will prefer newly minted spare parts when they can be made available. Those who can afford the best will be prepared to pay for the best.

Sooner or later it will occur to marketers that these biological parts do not have to be attached to our bodies. If legs work better than wheels, why not grow the legs independently and attach them directly to whatever has to be moved – the garden mower, for example? There is no law that robots have to be built of metal and silicon. Living tissue has a number of advantages. The non-natural creation of living artefacts is a little scary, but it has begun.

While the cloning of sheep has taken place, the cloning of complete people may never happen. From our perspective, it is not much of a commercial threat. International marketing depends on genetic diversity. Cloning people, as some over-standardized companies have discovered, reduces creativity and growth.

Supposing someone found a way to grow a (human-like) brain that worked more cost efficiently than a computer. Is that acceptable? Even if it had consciousness? This is not science fiction. Computer scientists are experimenting with organic materials. Micro-computers are being attached to patients with brain damage to enhance mental capacities. Live tissue could be more comfortable and less obvious and embarrassing for patients.

Biology is a young science. Darwin's theory of evolution and Mendel's laws of genetic inheritance were seen as contradictory for nearly a century until they were reconciled in the 1930s. The 1990s saw the beginnings of understanding the brain, thanks to electronic and magnetic imaging. Genetic engineering is a development of selective breeding techniques mankind has long practiced. We no more understand the long-term consequences of genetics than the nineteenth century understood that atomic science would lead to the atom bomb. Yet we cannot stop.

Philosophers have never been able to separate the ethics of the day from those that are timeless. Accordingly we cannot predict how these developments will be seen in the future when, or if, they emerge. What we do need is to adjust our thinking. The biological age is already taking over from the logical.

## Reducing the barriers of space and time

As we have discussed, time is a greater limiting resource for international management than money. Consumers can be divided into two groups: the money-rich/time-poor and the money-poor/time-rich. Both worry about the commodity they do not have. Our days are filled by distractions and we fight for the space to do what we want to do. We make time by performing separate tasks simultaneously. Driving to work, we shave/make up, have breakfast, and make a few phone calls. Harassed managers arrange time management meetings. Just as society is endangered by too large a gap between rich and poor, firms will increasingly need to pay attention to disparity in managerial time availability.

Much of this pressure is technology-driven. We can receive friends' holiday snapshots by e-mail from Disneyland or Aspen, and so we do. Supposedly time-saving technology takes more time when it is novel and when it goes wrong, but these are teething problems. Today's e-mail is no more unreliable than postal mail. On the other hand, technology is also shrinking distance and expanding time. The proportion of our lives spent in our main careers is shrinking. We are educated longer, leave home sooner and live longer. A doctor dictates notes in Ohio before going home; they are word-processed in Bangalore so they are back on the desk when the doctor arrives next morning.

West Coast consultant, Regis McKenna, sees consumer demands as being here and now.[3] They will not wait for shops to open nor travel to them.

Frances Cairncross of *The Economist* depicts the consequences of the communications revolution.[4] Size and location, in her view, will cease to matter, but brands will matter more. Organizations will be more loose-knit. Increased connectivity will spawn a multitude of ideas and better price information will lead to "better" markets.

In short, networks and the computer are changing our lives in ways both seen and unseen. "We are moving towards a network society rather than an employee society," wrote Peter Drucker.[5] Marketers need to understand this dispersed, impatient, spontaneous world. Take, for example, telephone systems that cost money and waste time with trivial options. They will have to go. They were installed to minimize staff time at the expense of user time. No one should have to speak to a computer except another computer. Empathy requires a deep understanding of customer and end user, present and future, activities in the four dimensions of time and space. Marketing advantage will go to those who develop this understanding.

## Implicit communications

Communication is more a matter of being connected than using those connections to pass specific messages. As any fine orator demonstrates, the spaces between words can be more important than the words themselves. Perhaps we will come to understand telepathy or maybe it is a myth. However it works, we know non-verbal communication is the critical stage in the creation of value.

If there is a single driver to freeing up time, it is the urge to be together with a social group. Telecommuting from home will be used increasingly, but it will not *replace* the need to be with the working team. Sorry, meetings will not go away.

*Non-verbal communication is the critical stage in the creation of value*

In the work context, the mechanization of information processing, transmission, and routines throws ironic light on what machines cannot do. We need each other in order to spark. Mozart needed an audience. Some of his finest improvisations, it is said, were triggered by the most responsive audiences.

Throughout this book we have given no explanation of how implicit communication works. We just know it does. Now we can speculate a bit and suggest that it has something to do with feelings, which, as you will recall, are co-located in the brain with social skill. We suddenly see a tranche of business books dealing with emotion.[6]

Digitizing has dramatically increased the amount of explicit information thrown at us. For example, the number of books published has more than doubled. This requires more filters to exclude whatever we feel (yes, feel) does not apply to us or is not important for us. These feelings act as gatekeepers to the messages we receive. Kevin Thomson, one of the new wave of writers on emotion in business, draws attention to the need to treat employees as internal customers and market to them accordingly. At present, firms are geometrically increasing the information they provide while, at the same time, the level of employee understanding of company policy is decreasing. These firms are relying on the explicit, and not the implicit, which, we are here suggesting, is closely linked with feelings and emotions.

Table 11.1 reproduces Thomson's Box which is his summary of the factors a board has to motivate and manage.[7] It bears more than a passing resemblence to the themes in this book.

**Table 11.1    Ten dynamic emotions in business**

- **Obsession** – persistent idea that constantly forces its way into consciousness
- **Challenge** – desire to rise up, fight and win – especially against the odds
- **Passion** – strong affection or enthusiasm for a product, service, personality concept or idea
- **Commitment** – the dedication to, or involvement with, a particular action or cause
- **Determination** – unwavering mind, firmness of purpose
- **Delight** – the act of receiving pleasure, such as fun, laughter, amusement
- **Love** – a great affection or attachment, to want to give
- **Pride** – feeling of honor and self-respect, a sense of personal worth and organizational worth
- **Desire** – wish to have, own or be
- **Trust** – confidence in the integrity, value or reliability of a person or entity, such as a team or organization

In short, feelings and implicit communications work together and have to operate *before* explicit information can be effective.

## New structures

Symbolic of Drucker's "network society" and the more "loose-knit" enterprise forecast by Cairncross, was the growth of the computer operating system, Linux, which now boasts more than 12 million users. As related by Malone and Laubacher, in October 1991 a 21-year-old computer science student at the University of Helsinki made a kernel of the Linux system available on the Internet.[8] He encouraged Internet users to download his software – for free – to use it, test it, and modify it as they saw fit. A few took him up. They fixed bugs, tinkered with the original code, and added new features. They, too, posted their work on the Internet. In time, the Linux community grew steadily, soon encompassing thousands of people around the world, all sharing their work freely with one another. Within three years, this loose, informal group, working without managers and connected mainly through the Internet, had turned Linux into one of the best versions of UNIX ever created.

This temporary, self-managed gathering of diverse individuals engaged in a common task, is a model for a new business organization, a self-regulating system that is forming the basis for a new kind of economy. The fundamental unit of such an economy is not the corporation, but the individual. Tasks are not assigned and controlled through a stable chain of management, but are carried out autonomously by independent contractors. These electronically connected freelancers – "e-lancers" – join together into fluid and temporary networks to produce and sell goods and services. When the job is done – after a day, a month, a year – the network dissolves. Its members again become independent agents, circulating through the economy, seeking the next assignment. In many respects, this describes the evolution of the Internet itself, as well as the rise of outsourcing and telecommuting. These trends point to the devolution of large, permanent corporations into flexible, temporary networks of individuals.

Rather than being held together by twentieth century notions of command and control, these networks will be joined by many intangible connections: social bonds, emotional attachments, trust and commitment. The "intangible" gains salience as organizations continue to flatten, dispersing authority to customer points, and decentralizing control. In this new environment of sometimes unclear definition, Miller depicts the organization as a chameleon, which "constantly adapts itself to its environment."[9] Drucker portrays organizations as inherently unstable because "they must be attuned for innovation, for the systematic abandonment of whatever is established, customary, familiar and comfortable …."

Accompanying this digital revolution is a social transformation that shifts the customary terrain of working relationships. The 1980s and 90s witnessed a major structural change between the generations in their willingness to respect formal authority. Younger generations demonstrate little tolerance of domineering superiors. They do not worry about cradle-to-grave job security in a traditional hierarchy. Their loyalty rests with team-mates, not with the corporation. During their careers, they will work for many employers. Organizations will compete for talent more on the basis of intangible values and aspirations than on the basis of traditional career paths, job security, and money – and it is exactly those person-centered values that blend with a PASSION culture.

How does all this impinge on the international marketer's job? It reinforces the need for internal marketing to build relationships and nurture the independent feelings of involvement, commitment and the rest of Thomson's list (*see* Table 11.1).

## Post-Cartesianism

Descartes placed reason, and thus humanity, at the apex of evolution. We are, or should be, rational. Choice-making was primarily a logical exercise, even if we did not understand why. In this vein, economists have employed more ingenuity in rationalizing human behavior than medieval theologians in proving the world was flat. Post-Cartesianism is distinguished by placing thinking within a context of affect and memory. Animal spirits are not, as Descartes believed, lower order behavior that contaminates the rational. The reverse is closer to the truth.

The relational perspective of marketing – empathy – does not treat humans as value-neutral, as transactional, utility maximizers, but as sentient, experiential beings. In this perspective, companies are social groups with economic consequences. To understand international marketing we need to humanize our perception of business. The world is a vast array of networks linking SILK to increase international and national marketers' understanding. These networks of relationships are conduits for animal spirits.

Keynes recognized the deficiency of an all-rational, all-cognitive economics discipline. He attributed investment decision making largely to those animal spirits. Descartes identified competing claims of affect and cognition and reversed their now apparent involvement in decision making. He also assumed that the two are more separable than they are. Thinking and feeling are highly interactive.

Photography, 100–150 years ago, sounded the death knell for representational art. The need for perfect imaging was no less. But the camera did the job better. The separation of imaging into photography and non-representational art was both evolution and revolution. This was not obvious at the time and the claim that modern art was displaced from presentation is open to challenge. We cannot know for sure, but it set a precedent for today.

A hundred years from now, our successors will similarly see the emergence of the computer as the end of the perception that decision making should be strictly rational, or cognitive. The need for quantitative techniques will not decline, but the computer will better fulfill that need. The computer is the ultimate Cartesian: it is bits, bytes, and central processing units undisturbed by animal spirits. As such, it is indeed the marketer's friend. As the computer takes on routine information processing and cognitive tasks, as it speeds our explicit communication needs, as it stores knowledge for instant retrieval and across global networks, the marketer is liberated for creative and relational activities. The arrival of the computer will displace international managers from purely logical functions just as the camera released the artist.

*The computer is the ultimate Cartesian: it is bits, bytes, and central processing units undisturbed by animal spirits*

We have considered marketing and doing business around the world from the perspective of the international manager. We have crossed borders of business function, academic discipline, cultures and, at times, even good taste. While borders help to frame issues, they can also obstruct learning; for example, Not Invented Here. Borders must be respected: they did not arise by chance. But a firm profits from its internationalism only to the extent that it takes advantage of the similarities between markets. Know-how is borderless and the future is biological.

*Know-how is borderless and the future is biological*

Connectivity in the new millennium will take place in ways we can only begin to imagine. In this book we have brought together connectivity in the brain (synapses and memory) and connectivity between people (relationships). One is analogue of the other; both are biological and both carry the traffic of global marketing. Whatever changes, PASSION will continue to drive business performance.

# References

1. Forster, E. M. *Howard's End*, Ch. 19.
2. Reported by Gould, S. J. (1999) in "It Takes More Than Genes to Make a Smart Rodent, or High IQ-Humans", *Time*, 13 September, p. 62.
3. McKenna, R. (1997) *Real Time*. Boston, Massachussetts: Harvard Business School Press.
4. Cairncross, F. (1997) *The Death of Distance*. London: Orion Business Books.
5. Drucker, P. (1992) "The New Society of Organizations", *Harvard Business Review*, Sept–Oct, pp. 95–104.
6. For example, Fineman, S. (1993) *Organisation as Emotional Arenas: Emotion in organisations*. London: Sage Publications.
   Goleman, D. (1996) *Emotion in Organisations*. London: Sage Publications.
   Thomson, K. (1998) *Emotional Capital*. Oxford: Capstone Publishing.
7. Thomson, *op cit.*, p. 24.
8. Malone, T. Laubacher, R. J. (1998) "The Dawn of the E-Lance Economy", *Harvard Business Review*, Sep–Oct.
9. Miller, D. (1997) "The Future Glory Organization: A chameleon in all its glory", in Hesselbein, F. *et al.* (ed) *The Organization of the Future*. San Francisco: Jossey-Bass.

# Index